THE OLD WEIRD ALBION

Justin Hopper is a writer concerned with landscape, memory and myth. His journalism, poetry, audio projects and curated exhibitions have appeared in both his native USA and adopted UK home. He lives in Constable Country with his partner and their son.

Mairead Dunne (ILLUSTRATOR) is an artist and illustrator based in the UK, having completed a MA in Fine Art and MA in Authorial Illustration. Working across a wide variety of mediums, she won the Michael Marks Illustrated Poetry Award 2016 for her work on *the clearing*, published by Atlantic Press.

The Old Weird Albion

Justin Hopper

with illustrations by Mairead Dunne

Penned in the Margins

LONDON

PUBLISHED BY PENNED IN THE MARGINS
Toynbee Studios, 28 Commercial Street, London E1 6AB
www.pennedinthemargins.co.uk

First published 2017

Printed in the United Kingdom by TJ International

ISBN
978-1-908058-37-9

CONTENTS

for Thomas

The Old
Weird
Albion

I BEGINNINGS

Landscape, Memory, Myth

ONCE THERE WAS A WOMAN who stood at the edge of a cliff. It was a sunny midsummer's Friday; a strong breeze brushed her skirt and troubled her hat. She looked out over the sea towards the south and an eternal, sun-drenched horizon. The woman had traveled all day to arrive at this place: a bus, a train, a walk alone to the cliff from the railway station with her handbag, her hat and little else. Boarding the train or walking up the hillside she still, instinctively, reached out for a tiny hand — there had been a child, now 18 months gone.

She looked down and saw the end of the land; recognized that she was an islander and that this horizon was the edge of her world. Perhaps she arrived at the cliff's edge without a plan. Perhaps she arrived at the edge, peered down the vertiginous strata at an archaeology of summer holidays and picnics; of traders, invaders and shipwrecks; of loves and losses and wanderings and home, and could go on no more.

In the blue haze of a summer afternoon, the green of the Downs rolling gently away from the white of the chalk, the cliff appeared peaceful. But it is the site of a crash, where the sine wave of an Old Road ceases to undulate and ceases to be. There are murmurs there, creaks and groans and wind whistles.

Once there was a woman who stood at the edge of a cliff, and when, finally, she let slip, she did not do so unseen. Holidaymakers and wandering locals watched in horror as she flew through the air and skipped along the jagged side until, 40 storeys below, she struck a ledge in the cliff. There, her body broken and torn, she hovered above the crash of blackened-blue waves on white chalk. There, she left a scar — a scorch mark, such as all lives leave in the landscape when they streak across it, or explode within.

§

At the edge The cliff was Beachy Head, near Eastbourne in Sussex. A 500-foot-tall lump of chalk peering out over the English Channel, Beachy Head holds a grim place in the English imagination, being one of Europe's most famous suicide spots. The woman was Doris Hopper, first wife of my grandfather, Bob Hopper. There is no word for the relationship Doris and I have — me, the product of her widowed husband's second marriage to a woman Doris never met. A few years ago I didn't even know for certain she had existed. No one I could speak to knew her name. And yet, 80 years after she went over that cliff, I felt compelled to seek out the traces of her life — and death.

I did so by walking. I walked the South Downs Way, the 100-mile footpath that stretches between central Hampshire and the English Channel at Beachy Head. The Downs — 'elevated rolling grassland', from the Old English word for hills, *dun* — form a naturally occurring pathway just north of the sea through West and East Sussex. I wish I could say that I had walked from Winchester to Beachy Head in a straight line, day after day, but that's not how it was; that's not how life works. The walks in this book took place over several years, some before I moved to England from my home in the northeastern USA, some after I had arrived and my son, Thomas, had been born. His birth added a new impetus to my quest: the need to understand Doris, who is a part of *his* family story, too; but more importantly, the need to understand England, the place he calls home.

This book tells the stories I encountered on my incursions into the Downs in the manner of nonfiction. But it is not journalism. It is a series of impressions that describe ways of relating to the landscape that both rely on and empower memory as an instrument of comfort. Sometimes that's through art or story, sometimes ritual or even magic. I will introduce you to the guides who showed me the paths and their meanings — some are living, many are long dead. They are all real people, although I have changed the names of some of them. The places and experiences are all true, but in a few instances more than one visit to the same location has been condensed into a single description.

In the course of these wanderings, I read the South Downs as a 'core sample' of another England. In this alternative zone that exists side by side with the modern world, the linear nature of time is not assured. There are places in the landscape that exude what might be called the 'everywhen'; they are haunted places. And ghosts require a little faith.

I grew up atheist in 1970s and '80s America, surrounded and fascinated by fanaticism. Just as many friends raised in the Church turned their backs on Catholicism or Methodism, I bristled against my parents' lack of religion, desperate to believe. At the same time, throughout my childhood, my father took us to England

— to Steyning in West Sussex, where my grandparents lived — and we would walk on the Downs. At some point these two childhood experiences converged. I began to look to the landscape for faith: I believed in its pull and its power. As I walked the Downs many years later, I was looking to experience that feeling again. I wanted to believe.

In the chapters that follow, I have sought out places where landscape intersects with memory and myth. Why do people find comfort in such sites? Doris was drawn to Beachy Head — as though some answer was embedded in the landscape. When someone disappears, when someone leaps from a cliff and is all-but-erased from memory, what traces might we find in the crumbling chalk of the cliff-face; in the wind that buffets the edge of this Albion?

II CROSSROADS

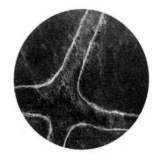

Searching for the Old Road and the River of Memory

TIME HAD GONE SOFT at the Crossroads, and let me tell you how. It was late afternoon and bright with spring sunshine; yet a ruddy, autumnal smell of bonfires and whisky rose from the earth. The land was bathed in a monochromatic acid trip; a nearby cluster of barrows glowed with psychedelic sepia tones. There was no one else around.

The Crossroads lies a few miles west of Amberley railway station in West Sussex, at a point on the South Downs triangulated by hamlets: Bignor to the north, Slindon to the south, Upwaltham further west. I walked alongside an unexpectedly busy road out of Amberley station and turned down a path towards a farm and a water-treatment plant. I encountered a bridge over the River Arun, a steep chalky incline, a field strewn with stones, but these landmarks weren't always visible at first: they rose up to meet the walker. Each patch of grass and ancient barrow emerged, awakening from the earth. I felt I was being held, as though every feature of the landscape was part of a gentle giant's palm. Everything cradled — sheep, thrush, walker — snug in its cupped hand. The road ran through it like a lifeline.

Besides the barrows — burial mounds left behind

by fairy folk or the devil — the dominant human-made features in this stretch of Sussex are paths. Just a dozen meters before the Crossroads I passed a car park with a signpost pointing in several directions at once, destinations named in English and Latin: Sutton, Slindon, Bignor, towns and villages nearby on the Downs; also Londinium and Noviomagus. At the Crossroads there's no such sign, just a confusion of crossing paths. I make up my own sign: Childhood, First Love, Sorrow, Joy.

The road I walked from Amberley, climbing from the Arun valley onto the Downs, is the sanctioned path between east and west — the South Downs Way. In the 20th century, the Way was designated as a single route: a line and a name on the map. But it has existed for thousands of years as a network of paths between Hampshire and the East Sussex coast. And the road's spine, its course and manner, were determined long before that by geology. Look at a relief map of the island of Britain and you can pick out the South Downs Way as a line of hilltops scored across the south coast. Time softens along that road because it follows a route embedded in geological, not human, experience.

At the Crossroads, the South Downs Way crosses

Stane Street, its younger cousin. Stane Street was the Roman road running north-south from Londinium (London) to Noviomagus Reginorum (Chichester). Whilst the Way is boot-made, the Street is a feat of engineering, raised earth and flat surfaces, a mirror of the geography of the Downs and the Weald. If the Way is a scrawled poem, Stane Street is an instruction manual.

It's there, where the engineered agger of Stane Street crosses the South Downs Way, in the burnt-umber glow, that I lay in the dirt and grass and chalk, dug my fingernails in, sinking down. From beside me came a haunted sound.

Stones in my pass-way

The voice was made shrill by the tinny speakers, mimicking the scraped guitar; a ghost's voice wafting across the thin border of time and space that exists at the Crossroads. Robert Johnson, the haunting memory of the American road. What did they think, the couple out walking, when their dogs ran to sniff in the long grass and discovered — not some hiker's discarded picnic — but six feet of American stretched out on the ground with demon-voiced Blues wailing beside him? *She* took in a quick startled gasp and then laughed. *He* looked annoyed and clapped at the dogs, calling them away from their new toys: my boots.

I had promised myself I would enact two rituals in this landscape, This was the first — a plea to my soul. I would sink into this ancient Crossroads with the patron devil-saint of the American road — saint of the 'hellhound on my trail', of 'waiting on a Greyhound bus', of 'stones in my passway'. For the second, a plea to my memory, I had another saint with me — pages in my pocket written by an Englishman with a French name: Hilaire Belloc, patron of Sussex walkers and poets, whose beer-splashed folktales might counterbalance Johnson's wild sermons. I'd take his pages and, following their instructions, wash my head in the Arun waters in the hope of forgetting everything I had known.

Lines on its face This landscape remembers. It remembers every footfall and wheel-roll; bears each of these as lines on its face, to be read and mapped and remembered by anyone who chooses.

I think of the South Downs as a 'core sample' from which we can extrapolate a narrative of this island's life. I wanted to find pockets in the Downs in which we can see another way of being. But to understand the South Downs, I had to understand chalk.

Chalk is a miracle. Among geologies, it is a Zen master. Chalk doesn't grip, it holds on loosely. Chalk breathes in water and air, purifying and sanctifying as it does. The chalk that comprises so much of southern England tells a long geological history of life in the ocean. Over millions of years, microscopic creatures consumed even tinier algae and deposited them as fossilized excrement, among which alighted fossil fish, sponges and other marine life, eventually creating white, porous mountains in the sea. In the Paleocene epoch, tectonic plates shifted in a massive global upheaval. Continents collided and those undersea chalk mountains were squeezed upwards like a pinched balloon, creating a giant ridge reaching from southern England across the Channel to Calais and the Artois region of France — the Weald-Artois Anticline.

Chalk is Zen

In England, the result of this event extends from the Sussex and Hampshire coastlines to the Medway. The ridge eroded away at its center over hundreds of millennia, leaving a long flattened plane between two chains of hills, the North and South Downs. The miles of forest that grew out of the erased middle is what we call the Weald.

Another curious thing about chalk: because it breathes water in and out, rather than soaking it up, these sets of hills remained dry, making them appealing routes across the landscape. When humans began farming the Weald as long as 10,000 years ago, the Downs became the perfect pathways between communities. They were dry year-round, with fantastic visibility in either direction, easy to defend and hard to get lost in.

As people began to farm and live on the Downs, the changes they made to animal and plant life made the land even more traversable. The tough scrublands were transformed into springy turf, and manmade dew ponds with chalk-purified water encouraged an abundance of life.

Thousands of years ago, drovers used the high, dry Downs to move their animals across the south of England. And by the time the Romans set foot on the chalk, the hills were settled. Rather than the sparse walker's paradise we know today, the Downs were speckled with hamlets. It wasn't to last. During the Middle Ages the population of the South Downs moved back down below. The escarpment became a guardian rather than a home.

But the Way remained, in concept and practice. According to historian Peter Brandon, 'it had been possible to walk from Beachy Head into Hampshire over pathless buoyant turf' until at least 1939. So in the 1930s, when the British government first acknowledged the possibility of drawing a constellation of interconnected paths together into a single national trail, it was as much about institutionalizing an existing practice as it was reviving a tradition.

The Way was officially designated in 1963, and opened for walkers as a complete 70-mile route in 1972: from the Hampshire village of Buriton, north of Portsmouth, to Eastbourne and the Seven Sisters. A decade later, that trail was extended 30 miles west to Winchester; in 2011, the South Downs National Park was opened, turning a swathe of the English map green. The extension to Winchester doesn't fit, geologically: the Downs themselves, the actual eruptions of chalk, begin to taper off closer to the original western border at Buriton and Old Winchester Hill. But this landscape remembers, and it remembers more than just chalk. It remembers footfalls and wheel-rolls all the way to Winchester and Salisbury Plain, once the center of the English universe.

The Old Road is comprised of all these things, from the fossils of algae and the weathered chalk anticline to the boots and wheels of Beaker people, Celts, Romano-Britons, Saxons, Normans: a living history of humans raising things up and stamping things down.

I saw the man sitting at the side of the path that leads from Amberley railway station to the South Downs Way. Even from a distance, I knew that we'd speak, knew that we'd part, knew that we'd someday meet again. He was crouched against the sun, breaking for water on a long walk.

"Walking the whole Way, or just out for the day?"

"Whole thing," he responded, standing up and extending a hand to meet mine. As he stretched his body, I could read the text — PAGANS AGAINST FASCISM — on his T-shirt. "Started yesterday morning from Winchester."

I noticed the sleeping bag rolled up on his pack. Wild camping. Making his way through the world. Adam — his name was Adam, of course it was — wasn't just 'outdoorsy'. He worshipped the landscape. He wouldn't walk much further that day, pulling up lame on top of the Downs between Amberley and Chanctonbury Ring, halfway to his home in Eastbourne. He would sleep there and encounter The Goddess; he would be spoken to and touched by the incarnation of it all. But that was yet to be.

"Yourself?"

"Just the day, walking out to Stane Street and then a quick dip in the Arun."

"Good day for it," he said. Wiped his brow. "I was considering it a few minutes ago."

"Are you familiar…" I screwed up my face, selling myself on a story I didn't entirely believe. "… with the *myth*?"

I told Adam the story about the Arun: that one who washes their head in its waters forgets everything they have seen since their 18th birthday. A reset button hidden in the landscape. He hadn't heard of it, but he understood the impulse. Perhaps, I thought, he might even understand my personal dilemma: belief and skepticism in equal parts.

I let Adam go — he had his own visions to get to — and climbed to the top of the next chalk hill, a steep one. There I stopped in the shade of a tree and from my back pocket I took a small book, held together with rubber bands and paper clips.

I first found Hilaire Belloc's *The Four Men* ten years before, on a visit from America to my grandmother's little house in Steyning, not far from Amberley. I was desperate for something to read and it was the only well-thumbed paperback on the shelf, a 1980s reprint. It collapsed open, the pages falling to the floor. The spine's glue had melted from a hundred flip-throughs. The first page I picked up was, to my delight, a list of pubs. Not just pubs, but pubs I knew: the Bridge Inn of Amberley, the White Horse at Storrington and its namesake in Steyning. This last had been my first English pub; it stood little more than 100 meters from the floor on which those pages were spread. And here it was in this funny little book written a century before.

At first I loved *The Four Men* because of its dedication to the things I craved at the time. Drink, song, walking. Later I came to recognize it as a work of walking-as-therapy, a couch session for a man in midlife crisis. Belloc splits his personality into four parts and takes them for a walk from Robertsbridge in the eastern Weald to his childhood haunts in the Arun valley. In what amounts to a 50-mile pub crawl, Belloc's archetypal characters — The Poet, The Sailor, Grizzlebeard and Myself — hold court on youth and age, philosophy and politics, memory and myth, and, of course, Sussex. These characters, conceived around the time of James Joyce's *A Portrait of the Artist as a Young Man*, are snared, time and time again, on what the Irish writer called 'those nets' — nationality, language, religion. These comprised Belloc's crisis of the time; he would encounter more, but these would do for the moment. The journey described by *The Four Men* allegedly took place in 1902, the year the French-born Belloc became a naturalized British citizen. The book was Belloc's attempt to stick a stake into Sussex ground, the place he'd known all his life yet of which he had only just been granted citizenship. Belloc had two homes, each with its own language, its own mask. A familiar feeling.

I flicked through my grandmother's copy of *The Four Men* until I found the appropriate page. A section around The Bridge Inn - I'd passed it after leaving the train station - and the Arun valley: I'd return to the river soon. I made a sheaf of pages, fallen or torn from the binding, to keep separate from the book and mingled them with a few I'd copied out of another of Belloc's books, *The Old Road* — another walk, again across Sussex. It was this that I eventually planted at the Crossroads, a balled-up piece of paper rambling about roads and fire and refuge: I placed it under a rock in the grass beside me.

'There are primal things which move us,' writes Belloc in *The Old Road*:

> Fire has the character of a free companion that has traveled with us from the first exile ... to hear two voices outside at night after a silence, even in crowded cities, transforms the mind. A Roof also, large and mothering, satisfies us here in the north much more than modern necessity can explain ... A Tower far off arrests a man's eye always: it is more than a break in the sky-line; it is an enemy's watch or the rallying defence to whose aid we are summoned. ... we craved these things — the camp, the refuge, the sentinels in the dark, the hearth — before we made them; they are part of our human manner, and when this civilization has perished they will reappear. Of these primal things the least obvious but the most important is The Road.

The road unites humankind. It cuts across the wilderness and keeps us close to one another; it is as vital as warmth, shelter, safety. It is an imperative, in Belloc's words, that keeps us 'from false journeys'. But *this* road — the one I was on, the one that crosses Stane Street, the one from Winchester to the sea at Eastbourne — this wasn't just a road; it was one of the Old Roads.

Belloc had a theory. There are, he says in *The Old Road*, five naturally occurring, raised pathways that lead, more or less, to Salisbury Plain: the North and South Downs, the Chilterns, Cotswolds, and Dorset Downs. Belloc argued that the roads came first: that the ancient seats at Winchester, Avebury, Stonehenge and their vicinity came to prominence in part because the area was the natural convergence of these geological formations. Belloc contended that the road led to the creation of an entire civilization, and he wanted to get down with it; to sink into that road.

> For my part I desired to step exactly in the footprints of such ancestors … I believed that, as I followed their hesitations at the river-crossings, as I climbed where they had climbed to a shrine whence they also had seen a wide plain, as I suffered the fatigue they suffered … something of their much keener life would wake again in the blood I drew from them.

I kept climbing, across a busy road and past a strange field covered entirely with stones — as though they were crops to be tended and harvested — and onwards, swirling around the chalk-lined path that seemed to travel ever-upwards. The Arun valley is deeply cut into the Downs; I

Dead voices gather

was ill-prepared. By the time I got to the Crossroads, I was ready to lie in the grass. I called up Robert Johnson on my phone and put it on one side; crumpled Belloc's ravings and weighed them down with a rock.

Whether a Crossroads is outside of Clarksdale or Tupelo or Amberley, the intersection of two long straight tracks means the Blues. Not SPONSORED BY BUDWEISER; no, the Crossroads is the place 'where dead voices gather'. Here I was, surrounded by all the decisions I hadn't made. The roads not taken, lingering in the air. This was the Crossroads of the poet Walt Whitman.

> You road I travel and look around!
> I believe you are not all that is here!
> I believe that something unseen is also here.

The river of Arun

It began to rain as I reached the western side of the bridge, a relief after the scorching sun, so I foraged for a sheltered spot where I might keep my pack dry. I was here to dunk my head in the River Arun in the hope of forgetting everything I knew.

It's a footbridge, but much larger than you're picturing, and enclosed by gates at either end in case a sheep or cow tries to make a break for it. I walked along the riverside and found a small platform of grass jutting out over the river, covered by a dome of leafy branches. I threw my pack beneath it and looked around.

The Arun is no mere picturesque stream: it runs deep and it runs quick. I scouted for dunking spots, but found nothing more suitable than where I'd parked my gear, so I pulled the white T-shirt over my head, took off my glasses and settled on my belly in the mud.

> The Sailor. 'Certainly we are bound for Arun, which, when a man bathes in it, makes him forget everything that has come upon him since his eighteenth year — or possibly his twenty-seventh.'
>
> 'Yes,' said Grizzlebeard, more gravely, 'we are bound for the river of Arun, which is as old as it is young, and therein we hope to find our youth, and to discover once again the things we knew.'

With some trepidation, I plunged my head and shoulders over the edge of the muddy bank and into the cold water.

My relationship with belief is befuddled: raised atheist, I wound up alternately embracing and scorning every religion, every superstition. Still unsure of what I think of God, I furtively heed the warning of almost any folktale or ghost story. So as I stood up and shook my head like a dog, for one moment I feared for what I had done.

Flashes came to me

And I remembered everything. Flashes came to me, my brain whirring through its drives, looking for missing blocks. Searching through years 18 and 19, I saw myself lying in bed, laid waste by mononucleosis and chicken pox, sated with codeine pills and '60s psych cassettes; the face of the police officer who picked me up after I'd been mugged and beaten on the city streets. I remembered, for the first time since it happened, the woozy, muddled state I felt coming out of the water after jumping in a river from a railway bridge, so out-of-place it was, so out of character. They were all still there, washing over, these moments of discombobulation, and one in particular.

A scene I've pictured a thousand times: a 13 year old crawls around the floor of the house he's lived in his entire life, arranging and rearranging model trains, Dungeons & Dragons figures and household items — paper-towel rolls, strawberry punnets — into an adventure playground for a pet mouse. The boy is home alone for the afternoon, a normal occurrence, and the big red rotary telephone rings, the kind of fire-alarm ring that stills everything — the boy and the mouse, a ticking clock, strangers walking past the open door.

What did my friend say when I answered that phone? That our mutual pal was dead? I sometimes think I can hear David saying down the line, *Joey's dead ... it was an accident ... cleaning his father's gun ... an accident ... he's dead, but it was an accident.* I hear it, in my memory, with David's voice, one I've known since before I can remember anything at all. It's as clear as the red telephone and the breezy June day. It was what I remembered then and it is what I remember now. But it is not, of course, what happened.

Four years later, graduating from high school, I overheard two classmates talking about a picture of that departed friend — dead by his own hand; a shotgun in the closet, terrified to reveal his scholastic failures. No mention of cleaning the gun, no mention of an accident. I interrupted my classmates, corrected them, and they corrected me back. I asked my friends, David, my family. My mother said she had explained what had happened, but I couldn't conjure it. To this day, I remember the sound of my

His own hand

friend's voice, telling me about the "accident"; I remember the sound of my mother confirming. My memory contains no facts of the incident, only myths I'd long ago stopped believing.

On the road we remember; along the river, we forget. Somewhere in between the two is the place we go in order to believe.

III SUBURBS

Mingling Memory and Myth in Peacehaven

I CLIMBED TO THE TOP of the double-decker bus. Robert nodded me on. "Right to the back," he said, "where the cool kids sit." Our journey from Brighton Pier to Peacehaven was only six miles. Each mile conjured another village: Kemptown, Rottingdean, Saltdean and, eventually, the well-shorn lawns and bungalows of Peacehaven itself. It was there that my father first moved after the War. The suburban bus routes of Sussex mapped his family's life from then on: Peacehaven to Moulescoomb to Shoreham-by-Sea.

Robert was a native of Peacehaven, though he had long since moved to the county town of Lewes. He had the look you'd expect of someone forged in the space trapped between Downland and sea — dewpond eyes and peppered gorse hair. I'd met Robert through folk music. He was a fine tenor with a deep knowledge of traditional songs, and often sang before headliners at the local folk clubs. He was surprised to hear that I (or anyone) had an interest in his hometown, a place few tourists visit. I assured him it was important to me, and Robert agreed to "show me the sights".

We began to walk along Roderick Avenue, a wedge of a road that splits Peacehaven in two as if to reveal its inner workings. Roderick began as a stone-inlayed dirt path beside a chain-link fence beside the cliffs. From there, we headed north, and Roderick expanded — from domestic trickle to wide suburban avenue.

As we passed 3 Roderick Avenue, I thought back to 1998. At the end of that year, a young barmaid named Tiffany Mitchell met a bitter end, driving her car frantically into oncoming traffic. She died at the scene of the accident. After her cremation, Tiffany's ashes were taken from east London and scattered over the cliffs at Peacehaven, where she had spent many happy holidays. And it is to Peacehaven that Tiffany's fans came to grieve, visiting 3 Roderick Avenue—the house where she spent those joyful summers. They stopped by the pub garden in which she dined, and the beach on which she played, all part of the town's Tiffany Tour.

Like many aspects of Peacehaven's history, none of this is real — including Tiffany Mitchell herself. As one of TV soap opera *Eastenders*' most popular characters, Tiffany required a final resting place and accompanying backstory. Peacehaven worked perfectly because mashing up myth and reality is a role Peacehaven relishes. Within a year of Tiffany's death, local residents had fleshed out her story, arbitrarily assigning locations for her idyllic childhood.

Tiffany Mitchell is the ideal Peacehaven resident. The town's neatly arranged rows of houses are built from a mish-mash of architectural digressions. Like an American suburb, Peacehaven's streets carry the names of that which was destroyed to clear their way: Sheepfold Close, Hairpin Croft, Badgerfield. But even some of the sheepfolds and crofts were never there. In the shadow of the Downs, Peacehaven's creators developed a backstory for their idyllic location. Then they destroyed it and built a suburb.

As Robert led me up Roderick Avenue, we passed the G_d Companions sports bar, where they'd managed to hang a dozen England flags all around for an upcoming football match but not bothered to replace either 'o' from 'Good.' Just beyond it, Robert pointed to an imposing structure. "The locals used to call it 'Colditz'. I'm not sure if there's an 'anti-ugly-architecture' terrorist group, but if there is, I'd nominate this as a target."

Balcombe Court was a multi-building plaza of inhumane living quarters and business square footage that lived up to its reputation. Balcombe — or 'Ba'combe' thanks to a missing *l* — was an imposing mess of exposed antennae and satellite dishes stretching from window to rooftop. Its component parts stood at different, apparently random, heights, a design feature that made it at once bunker and guard tower; a nice place to wait out a wide variety of apocalypses. In the background, the grassy stoop of the Downs — not more than half an hour's walk. Ba'combe was typical Peacehaven, carved out of nothing with the force of will.

Pros-trate with dismal

My father and his family, like many Peacehavenites, arrived in the town in a rush after the Second World War. Peacehaven was built to facilitate reinvention. In the early part of the 20th century, Charles Neville of Darlington made a small fortune the old-fashioned way: he robbed the natives. Having traveled to Australia, the enterprising Englishman bought a schooner and sailed to New Guinea. There, he bought resource-rich land at dirt-cheap prices from the natives, sailed back to Australia, and sold the land at a decent profit.

In 1912, Neville returned to England and began poking around for a similarly promising possibility. On the south coast, near the farming village of Rottingdean, he found what would be his answer by the site of a Bronze-age burial mound in the parish of Piddinghoe, on the cliffs between the Downs and the sea. Neville's site was only half a dozen miles east of rapidly expanding Brighton, but far enough, and picturesque enough, for it to appeal to those who longed for a piece of Albion to call their own. He quickly bought up acreage in the area, organized a company to develop the land and concocted a scheme to populate it.

Walking up Roderick Avenue I was struck by the vagaries of its architecture. Houses alternately crouch low from the sun and rise against the wind. Their structures are of false flint, false stucco, false thatch. One example had a false-brick exterior and Mediterranean-tiled roof; timber farmhouse window shutters with iron hinges and clovers carved into them; a front garden of petunias, palm trees and CCTV. Despite uniformity among the land allotments and the time of erection (almost nothing predates 1915), Peacehaven seems to have sprung from a hundred different eras and attitudes.

The embryonic town was populated like an American land rush via a contest in the *Daily Express*. Contestants won parcels of land, and once they had the land, there were few rules as to what they built on it. The new inhabitants took full advantage of this lawlessness. To the people living and working on the farms that surrounded it, Peacehaven's development was like a bomb going off in reverse. As the Rottingdean folk singer and farm worker Jim Copper watched Peacehaven appear, he lamented, "'Ouses, 'ouses, 'ouses … it makes me prostrate with dismal."

The contest, held as the Great War raged on, asked entrants to help name the new town. In honor of the Australia and New Zealand Army Corps and in memory of Gallipoli, the winning entry was 'New ANZAC-On-Sea'. Neville advertised that the winner and a limited number of runners-up were to win parcels of beachfront land valued at £50. Newspapers reported winners up and down Britain, excited by the new life that awaited them after the war.

As it turned out, that 'limited number' of runners-up included *every entrant* — an estimated 3,000 people — with the sole requirement that they pay 3 guineas to cover fees. Those who paid and traveled to Sussex to visit their land discovered things weren't quite as they'd imagined, as reported in the *Birmingham Gazette* in 1916.

The plots they were to receive were to contain about 250 superficial feet, but the evidence would show that the estate was absolutely derelict. *You could not get down to the beach, and if you did, there was no beach*, declared counsel. The cliff was continually falling, and if you did get down to the seashore it was dangerous to remain there.

Lawsuits were settled. Within a year Neville had unilaterally rejected the contest's results and changed his town's name to Peacehaven.

"It's a name from the dawn of the age of double-speak," said Robert. "There was never a 'haven' anywhere near here — and if there were, it certainly wouldn't be peaceful."

Double-speak, maybe, but it was a falsehood that suited interwar Britain. Twenty years after its founding, Peacehaven had already become a code word for the moral uncertainty of edgelands suburban life — life between the city and the countryside, in the places of forgetting and reinvention. In his novel *Brighton Rock*, Graham Greene uses the town as a dark turn on the Shakespearean forest — the marginal space to which his anti-hero, Pinkie, retreats to work out the problems of the modern world.

'Where'll we go Pinkie?'

'Somewhere,' Pinkie said, 'out in the country. That's where people go on a day like this.' He tried to think for a moment of where the country was: the racecourse, that was country; and then a bus came by marked Peacehaven, and he waved his hand to it. 'There you are,' he said, 'that's country. We can talk there. There's things we got to get straight.'

[...]

Little tarred bungalows with tin roofs paraded backwards, gardens scratched in the chalk, dry flower beds like Saxon emblems carved on the downs. ... hundreds of feet below, the pale green sea washed into the scarred and shabby side of England. Peacehaven itself dwindled out against the downs: half-made streets turned into grass tracks.

Roderick Avenue is the path that leads to Peacehaven's dwindling-out; the shabby cliffs still bookend this purgatorial scene — the place England goes to forget. In the climactic scenes of *Brighton Rock*, we return to Peacehaven's cliffs. A struggle ensues, and anti-hero Pinkie goes over the edge:

'Stop him,' Dallow cried; it wasn't any good; he was at the edge, he was over; they couldn't even hear a splash. It was as if he'd been withdrawn suddenly by a hand out of any existence

— past or present, whipped away into zero — nothing.

Yet, as Greene implies in the aftermath, not *quite* nothing. The discarded, the renamed, the reinvented, the absent and forgotten — they always leave a trace.

At the cliffs there had been a busy town's drone of horns and shouts; soon, this gave way to bedroom-community warbling — the floating hum of a residential main drag. Further on, even the twitchers of the retirement side streets, clipping occasional dandelions and watching to ensure we kept off their lawns, were inaudible, surrendering to birdsong and wind-groan. At this point, we were closer to the fields than to the town's center. Time began to blur. Was this the Britain of the Blitz or of Brexit, or some 'everywhen' that has always been, a connective tissue between the two?

The dwin-dling out

I was reminded of two artworks: Frank Newbould's undulating hills and white chalk, shepherd and flock and farmhouses nestled amongst the Downs, bearing the legend YOUR BRITAIN — FIGHT FOR IT NOW, painted and distributed to rouse men into action during the Second World War. And Keith Arnatt's *A.O.N.B.* photographs, black-and-white images of rubbish piles and abandoned camper vans beside the River Wye, along the one-time must-do walk of the English picturesque. The juxtaposition of a teardrop-stirring English countryside and the normal life from which we view it. That was Peacehaven at the point of its dwindling out.

Into the pit

We turned right onto Firle Road and headed east. Firle is an ancient beacon-point on the South Downs that beckons from the north, and Firle Road is one of the roads that leads to the end of Peacehaven, emptying into a field by Hoddern Farm. Robert's stepfather owned two houses on Firle Road in the 1950s. Firle Road is also where my father lived as a child a few years before Robert. Robert's friend David lived at Hoddern Farm. He was that most sought-after kind of '50s pal: the kind with a television. "There was a show on called *Quatermass and the Pit*," Robert said, pointing up the road as though Quatermass himself lived at its end. "To a child in 1958, it was the most terrifying thing you could watch. And every Monday night, after it finished, I'd have to walk back down the path and a pitch-dark Firle Road to get home."

In the 1950s, Professor Bernard Quatermass

contributed a new archetype to the pantheon of England's defenders of the realm. Alongside armored crusaders, the Thin Red Line and the chain-smoking Tommy, now stood The Boffin: the scientist whose bouncing bombs and portable docks had defeated Jerry and kept England free.

Screenwriter Nigel Kneale's *Quatermass* began in the grand tradition of American sci-fi serials — hero-saves-world-from-alien-invasion-but-is-just-doing-his-job, even if, in this case, that hero is British brains rather than Yankee brawn. But the postwar mood was changing. By the time of *The Pit*, *Quatermass* had shifted its scope: the enemy was to be found within. It took a basic premise of film noir — that the hero is also, somehow, implicated in the crime — and magnified it out of all proportion: we carry the enemy within our DNA.

In *Quatermass and the Pit*, our hero is called to a Knightsbridge Tube station (the fictitious Hobbs Lane) in the years after the war. What was originally thought to be an unexploded German bomb turns out to be a Martian spaceship. The ship leads Quatermass to discover a terrible secret about aliens, humans, and where the two have met before.

After the spaceship is excavated, the people working

and living around Hobbs Lane begin experiencing hallucinations, strange dreams and hauntings. Quatermass interviews the oldest residents, and discovers that this isn't the first time ghosts have invaded. It had happened when the station was first excavated 30 years before, and from historical records, it seems to have been a regular occurrence for centuries.

As the Professor discovers, Hobb is a name which had been associated with the Devil right back to the Middle Ages and before. In *Quatermass*, these place names and the supernatural phenomena associated with them are manifestations of a deep-rooted memory — we can't directly interpret them, but they act as breadcrumbs for understanding the meaning of that place; a meaning a place can never escape. We can rearrange the name, reword it, retell the story with a different middle, but the end is always the same. As cartographer Tim Robinson has argued, 'A place name is a few words piled up to mark a spot; a few stones that fall down after some generations, perhaps for someone else to pile them up again into a different shape.'

In *Quatermass*, the spot being marked holds the memory of a great racial cataclysm: an alien invasion meddling with the DNA of our pre-human ancestors. This cataclysm is commemorated not only in place names but in other memories — for example the common, horned image of the devil, which mirrors the insect-like visage of our alien masters. And the ghosts of a terrible moment in human history, forever haunting the landscape in which that cataclysm occurred.

Robert walked Firle Road lightly, on cat-burglar's toes. He stopped in front of an inconsequential-looking building at an intersection with another residential avenue. The building was a creamy, broad-shouldered monolith that loomed over its squat neighbors. Robert pointed to one of the bruise-like PVC windows. *Away from those ghosts*

"There was a ghostly, pale figure that would appear suddenly in *Quatermass*," Robert said. "Every time I walked past this window right here, I was terrified of seeing that figure. Yet I could never look away."

Built in 1923, Long Stones is the kind of conceptual structure that Peacehaven summons into being. Surrounded by standard-issue bungalows and self-built suburban paradises, Long Stones was designed as a castle, complete with turrets and ramparts, now long removed, just scars on the building's face. By the 1950s, it had passed into the hands of a colonel and his wife, whom he called 'Mummy.' (Without a description of the homeowner I paint him as Colonel Mustard or Major Gowen, face crowded with mustache and red with colonial bluster.) After several happy years' retirement in the civility of Peacehaven, Mummy passed away, and, so it seems, she took a bit of the Colonel's mind with her.

Robert's mother had the unenviable job of housekeeper to the Colonel, and young Robert would spend many days helping to care for, and clean up after, the aging officer. He had left the front room on the ground floor - Mummy's room - untouched, exactly as it had been the day she died.

"I'd be there, playing, or watching the television, or helping around the house as my mother worked," said Robert, pointing to each room as he stated its purpose. "But I could hardly walk past the outside of that front room — nevermind go in. Sometimes, the Colonel would grab my shoulder with a smile and whisper, 'Today's a special day, Robert — Mummy's coming for a visit tonight.'"

It wasn't too long before the Colonel joined his

wife. Long Stones' rooms were divided up, and it became Serendipity, an unfortunately named hospice for people suffering from dementia. But Serendipity, too, was not to last.

As Robert and I loitered, the door to Long Stones opened and a woman stepped outside to light a cigarette. She drew upon it heavily, like an athlete with an oxygen mask. She was dressed in track pants and a loose shirt, her hair tied back in a utilitarian ponytail. We were standing across the street with heavily loaded backpacks, photographing and staring at this unattractive false-stuccoed building as though it were the Houses of Parliament. She probably thought we were terrorists. We nodded to one another, agreeing, silently, that the best policy was to approach.

"Excuse me," enquired Robert. "Do you live in this building? I lived in Peacehaven as a child, and am showing my American friend parts of the town that were here when I was."

"Oh." She was flustered. "Yeah — well, at the moment."

"May I ask, is it flats now?"

"It's…" She paused and looked at her slippers. "It's

temporary housing. It's owned by the Council."

A cat leapt onto the window ledge inside Mummy's front room, and I jumped slightly. Robert, too.

We continued towards the Farm, away from those ghosts and towards others. It's hard to escape, this England; there are so many ghosts, so densely populating the houses, the earth. When we pass by a place, loiter beside it, more so when we live our fiery lives within it, that place retains some trace of our passing. But perhaps a place like Long Stones — a place on the edge in more ways than one — can do more than just retain a memory like an imprint. Perhaps it can take that memory away for a while, in exchange for what we need at the time, like a pawnshop. Long Stones, like Peacehaven itself, attracts people who need to forget. A fortified castle in which to workshop a new name or build a whole new backstory — of peaceful times and happy holidays in a haven by the sea.

IV SEARCHING FOR DORIS

Part One

DORIS HOPPER ENTERED MY LIFE as a throwaway
comment. She, the woman at the edge of the cliff, was
my grandfather's first wife. They had a happy home and a
child together, but a decade after my grandfather's death
little was known about her but speculation and rumor.
Even her name was a mystery. "I think he was married
before," a relative said of my grandfather, Bob Hopper.
And then, nothing: no further information, barely even a
story. Something had happened. But what? She was taken
ill. Or was she struck by a car? No. Beachy Head: someone
was sure that she had thrown herself off Beachy Head.

It must have been between the wars. My grandfather
married his second wife, my grandmother, in 1937, so
Doris Hopper came into the picture in the 1920s —
the last gasp of a world from which one could utterly
disappear. It was the topic of so much concern at the time:
how do we establish a sense of identity, of order, in a world
governed by chaos and bounded by the unknowable?
Doris was of that world, the one born out of the Great
War. The generation that fell between the cracks.

I tucked Beachy Head into the back of my mind, but it
crept out at night, the woman on the edge appearing to

me in period costume. But it was the wrong period. When I imagined her, it was as the headmistresses in *Picnic at Hanging Rock*, the wrong time, wrong nation, wrong age. But, still, she was there. My grandparents were dead, as were their peers, and I sometimes had the romantic notion that I was the only one thinking of Doris.

I began to include Doris in my walks across the Downs, taking her with me as I looked for signs. The contours and brackets of her life began to come into view. Even with only droplets of knowledge about her, there were historical parameters; ranges of dates, limited geographies in which to look; a few facts I could jot down on a napkin. She had begun as an unknowable entity, but with a few bits of mathematics, she began to take shape.

Robert Hopper, my grandfather, was born in 1902, a member of the Interbellum generation: too young for the First World War, too old for the Second. Today we'd think of them as lucky, but those men often felt the opposite. As a young man he was fierce of temper and energies, and his relatives said he would've been first over the top every time, certain to be mown down. After Bob's death in 1983 it was said of him that had he been born a few years earlier, none of us would be here.

His life's work, however, didn't display such passion. As a young man Bob took a job as a clerk in a bank. He stayed in the field all his life, moving from good, boring job to good, boring job. He had been born in Lewisham to a warehouse laborer from a line of industrial workers. But Bob's dad had risen to become a traveling salesman and moved to the suburbs — Croydon, Surrey. It must have been impressed upon young Bob that a steady job with decent pay and no chance of being crushed to death was textbook success. And how could such 20th-century suburban success be conjured without a wife? Bob's life must have come into focus mid-1920s, and a wife was part of that equation.

Sure enough, a digital record eventually appeared in my searches. On 16th April 1927, Robert Hopper married a woman named Stubbins in Lewisham, southeast London. The first piece of the puzzle was slotting into place. Stubbins — probably an error, I thought. It must be 'Stubbings'. I asked a few people in my family, but no one knew that name. The shadow remained until a greenish-yellow piece of paper arrived in the post; on it a mimeograph-like facsimile of handwriting nearly 90 years old. She was, I discovered, a secretary from Wandsworth, and she was also the daughter of a traveling salesman. Her name was listed on the Marriage Certificate as 'Dorothy Florence Stubbings or Doris Florence Greenin'. So I mentioned the new name to my father and he gasped over the phone: "Goodness — Mrs Greenin?"

With-drawn by a hand When my father, Paul, was a small boy, during the war, he and his brothers and a few other family members were evacuated from their home in south London to the small village of Ilfracombe on the North Devon coast. On one of the first nights there, among the first that toddler Paul had ever spent outside of the city, there was a thunderstorm. In the morning the host family had asked, "Were you scared of the storm last night, Paul?"

"No, I just pulled my blanket over my head and pretended it was bombs."

At Ilfracombe, my father remembered, there was another woman who had accompanied them — an older woman who helped care for the kids and the house. The children didn't know much about her, or at least didn't remember 70 years on, but my father did recall her name: Mrs Greenin. Doris's widowed mother. By the time of the war, her first husband, named Stubbings, and her second,

Greenin, were both dead. Her children were dead, too, or unaccounted for. By 1947 she too would be gone, leaving her pittance to my grandfather's family, which had, by then, become *her* family.

The night after receiving the marriage certificate and talking to my father, I went to bed thinking about erasure. Doris Hopper née Greenin née Dorothy Stubbings had removed herself from history so effectively. And what about Beachy Head?

There was still no piece of paper confirming Doris's fate. The first marriage was real. Doris was real — here she was, in black-and-yellow-green. There were even the beginnings of a memory: my father had met her mother, almost certainly had been cradled in her arms. There was so little remove and yet she was so far away, almost another dimension. She was a glitch in the timeline.

Doris's fate was like Pinkie's: 'It was as if [she'd] been withdrawn suddenly by a hand out of any existence — past or present, whipped away into zero — nothing.' But, like Pinkie, of course that wasn't true. There were stories — marks, traces — that Doris left behind, she, the woman at the edge. I just needed to keep looking for documents, and to keep listening when she visited my dreams.

v ANTIQUITIES

Trespassing at the Druid's Stone

A MASSIVE STANDING STONE loomed above us, nearly twenty feet tall and half as wide at its base. Footholds carved into the side led up to a smoothed top. And cut into the entire height of the stone was a perfect sluice a foot deep and a few inches wide, providing a natural gutter for the day's heavy downpour. Simon smiled at me, in equal parts proud father and vindictive coach.

"Go on. Climb."

So I did. I tucked camera and notebook into my slickened waterproofs and reached out for the cold, wet smoothness of the carved steps. But despite the rain, the water pooling on the stone was lukewarm. A miracle — what else could it be? — and a sign that I should go on. Messages and miracles were everywhere here, riding the ley lines of deep Sussex, if you knew how to read them — or traveled with someone willing to explain.

Each step required a sharp breath of concentration, swiveling on the balls of my feet, arching for position. My hands were constantly scratching at smooth stone above, but there was nothing to grip. Simon's gaze solidified into beams of pure judgment and I found myself trying to act naturally. I was halfway up a frictionless sacrificial stone and making a meal of it.

Then, a few stretched limbs later, Simon and Mick were out of sight. All around me was a shroud of drooping woods — no sound but the rain, no sights but the gauzy thickness of leaves and bark. Like a child fumbling nervously up the high-dive at a public pool, it was only when I reached the top that I lifted my head and felt the swirl of adrenaline and calm. From the flattened altar top I could see mile after mile, but the fence we'd climbed, the NO TRESPASSING signs we'd ignored, the blurry villages we'd raced through, they were all gone.

From the top of the stone, I looked out onto a land that I had never seen before. It was Jaffa orange and ember-glow red and pebble blue and, most of all, whole palettes of greens — moss green, juniper green; fern and forest. I could almost reach out and touch the textures of the land, the thorny snatches of conifer, deciduous clumps, the pools of stone and still water. It was oceanic. Each individual plant or pond or stone was subsumed by the whole.

When I eventually climbed down, I thought I had been up there for hours. That other world I knew, the normal world, was still out there — of course it was. But in those minutes, it had seemed impossible that they could coexist. And once I came down, I didn't want it to be so. I wanted everything to be swallowed by those juniper greens and dewy ferns, including me. My guides, Simon and Mick, had told me they were taking me to a place they would only call "Happy Valley" — a trite name I took for a gag. But on the standing stone, I was there.

I had forgotten that the spot on which I'd perched was a sacrificial altar. At least, that's the story — there's no definitive archaeological proof that the blood of humans offered to the old gods had flowed through that sluice. But two things of which I can assure you with absolute certainty: one, the wild-eyed conspiracy theorists I was with thought that to be the case; and, two, they were the only people on earth who knew where I was.

I first met Simon at the Colonnade Bar in Brighton. Simon had informed me that he and his crew of 'archaeo-astronomers' and antiquarians knew all there was to know about the earth energies, standing stones and secret histories that kept Sussex moving on an astral level. Before I had a chance to ask, Simon suggested we meet up for a walk. Maybe, he said, he could even get his friend Mick to join us. Mick was "the real thing". Authentic. Connected

The old gods

to the old ways.

I would not have picked Simon out at the Colonnade Bar. I was expecting Peruvian headwear and a beard tied in a twist. At least a Hawkwind T-shirt. But Simon had cropped salt-and-pepper hair, gold chains and camouflage trousers. His gruff Cockney accent brought to mind East End cabbies and Columbia Road flower merchants. He leaned against the Colonnade's bar rail and let his eyes skip past the real ales to the cold, strong continental lagers. I'd met 'Simons' before; not at Brighton hippie gigs or on a country stroll, but in the Boleyn pub before West Ham home games.

Simon was a child of London, but a stepchild of Glastonbury. A festival kid who loved music and adventure, with the odd chemical to help fire up either one. His revelation had come when he and his girlfriend had embarked on an around-the-world trip, taking in the mysteries of earth and sky in India, the Himalayas, and remote Pacific islands.

"Where I've been truly blessed is that I've been able to travel."

Simon's words packed a glottal punch that he accentuated with palm-smacks to the bar. "I've been to the

Far East and the Pacific and..." *Whack!* "... out into the jungle with the machete! And after that, I've come back here and seen this landscape with renewed eyes.

We've always been led to believe our ancestors were dragging their knuckles before the Romans saved us from ourselves. But the people of Britain had knowledge we don't even know of now. What we want to do is reawaken that knowledge, keep it alive, for whatever purpose may come."

Today's rogue antiquarian is best described not with the scientific language of archaeologists or anthropologists nor the object-mania of the collector-hoarder, but in the *lingua franca* they share: Science Fiction. In Philip K. Dick's short story 'Paycheck', a man wakes up to discover he's traded all his wealth for an envelope of banal objects: a bus token, a used ticket stub, a broken casino chip. He soon discovers that he is in grave danger, hounded and threatened at every turn, and at the crucial moment of every peril, his envelope contains the object he needs to escape. He had seen his own future and left a legacy that would make survival possible.

To Simon, the standing stones and ley lines, the

Sticks, shadows, paces

myths and legends of the South Downs landscape, are all objects left to us by our forefathers. Stone circles? Psychic flying buttresses. Ley lines? The geological lifelines we will cling to in an environmental apocalypse. Is Stonehenge none of the things proposed by archaeologists, but, instead, the solution to a danger we've not yet encountered?

This vision of the British landscape is by no means new. It is a long-held New Age belief that there is invaluable knowledge once held by our pre-industrial ancestors that we have since lost. Fortunately, the theory also holds, those ancestors knew that we'd forget. So they left us a series of reminders in the landscape — physical artifacts, like stone circles and burial mounds, but also cultural ideas that manifest themselves as place names and collective memories: folk tales, songs, legends. Every now and then, in those pockets of the country untouched by modernity, the confluence of those ideas pops up in a single person.

A few years before I met them, at an autumn equinox in the mid-2000s, Simon's crew tried their hand at building a new stone circle on the South Downs. Using nothing but "sticks, shadows and paces", they plotted out

the circle in a ceremony called Drawing Down the North
— a ritualized mapping of the cardinal points performed
under a clear, starry sky. They aligned their circle to the
rising and setting sun, and celebrated with a weekend of
camping and music. To sanctify their new addition to
the prehistoric landscape, rather than a ribbon-cutting
politician or hard-hatted chairman, they chose Mick.
White-haired, rail-thin, he stood inside the circle and
called on the rooks. One of the birds answered Mick's call
and, to prove that the circle was good and true, landed in
its center.

The interior of Mick's beaten-up station wagon was *As-cended masters*
filled with a warm, awful fug. Frequently he reached
forward, wiped off a section of windshield no larger than
a hardback book, and resumed at breakneck speed along
the anonymous single-lane country roads. Occasionally,
we pulled to a complete stop, Mick tugged his thick specs
from under his long white hair and rubbed them with a
drenched bit of shirt. We splashed across fords ankle-deep
in rainwater, and were turned back more than once. I
jotted down village names and landmarks, where I could
see them, in a vain attempt to follow our path: Ardingly

and West Hoathly, Horsted Keynes railway station and the old gallows site of Wyche's Cross. But for the most part all I saw was a blur of houses and trees, a breath-steamed window.

Even driving blind and wet and skittish, Mick inspired confidence. Maybe it was the Marlboro Light dangling from his mouth, like a cowboy, or the calm with which he made even the most dangerous maneuver. Mostly, it was because the Downs and Weald are Mick country. He knew this territory better than most of us will ever know anywhere. For more than half a century he had struck out and receded back into it, a guerilla fighting an occupying army with his old, weird spirituality. Simon scowled at the chain pubs and zebra crossings as we passed through picturesque villages populated by politicians and their wealthy psychotherapists. To Mick, the modern world was an invasive species. His Sussex lived on quietly beneath it.

Mick was born in 1946 on a farm near the border where Sussex, Kent and Surrey meet. Mick's father worked the manor farms of mid-Sussex all his life, and Mick spent his days alternately playing on and working these lands. When I first met him, he was hunched over a cup of tea in Simon's Brighton apartment. The flat was small and chaotic, littered with the objects of Simon's two children: toys, clothes and picture books. Beneath that, signs of something that had come before: photos of ancient sites in the Himalayas, snapshots of Simon and his partner in a field at Glastonbury Festival, her pregnant belly sketched with runes. And scattered amongst it all: maps, globes, dowsing rods, crystals — the lot.

Mick leaned against the small kitchen counter. ("Sorry, no surnames," Mick told me. "If you use my last name, or even my real first name, then *they* can trace me.") Rumpled plaid flannel draped over a denim-blue cotton shirt. Black jeans and a Jack Daniel's belt buckle hanging loose from a waifish waist. Complete with a warm, toothless smile, Mick would have fit in at any rodeo or NASCAR race.

"I first ascended in 1972," Mick told me within minutes of our first introduction. "That's when I first spoke to the elders. In outer space."

Simon had warned me that Mick was an "Ascension Master", but I hadn't understood the implications. Mick's connection with the Earth had reached an almost divine status. His knowledge of the landscape mysteries of southern England came directly from the source: twelve vibrational beings that comprise a form of pure energy, and who allow the likes of Mick to receive (or "download") information.

Based in theosophy, but reaching out to a complex web of Eastern and Western mystical ideas, the Ascended Master is, essentially, the gumbo of esoteric traditions. The Ascension Masters I read about later screamed pyramid scheme. But Mick's version boiled down to one simple thing: an understanding of our human relationship to the landscape. It was couched in a lot of strange language, but the idea made a kind of sense to me.

I shook Mick's outstretched hand.

"Sounds like I've come to the right guy."

At this, Mick grinned and began speaking to Simon about where they should take me for the day. The Earthship at Stanmer Park? The ancient fort at Lodge Hill? Or perhaps East Grinstead, "center of all religion on Earth"? I never heard the answer, but I got in the car.

Straight tracks Mick held a staff between his thumb and forefinger, raised like a helicopter blade above his head. "You don't need dowsing rods," he said, nodding towards Simon. "All you need is a good piece of metal or wood - this one's just a sawn-off broom handle."

A few feet away from us, Simon was creeping around the church, counter-clockwise. In each hand was an L-shaped metal rod about a foot long with a black plastic handle. One of these dowsing rods was pointed down at his side, while the other was held close to his chest, aimed forward, the way Humphrey Bogart might hold a gun. Simon cut a professional figure.

The subject of his investigation was the outer wall of St Mary Magdalene church in the small village of Coldean. Mick and Simon had been itching to dowse the church for months. They believed it to be on a powerful ley line running out of Brighton near the Lewes Road, and they wanted to map out its earth energies.

In the early 20th century, topographer Alfred Watkins had proposed that Britain was once criss-crossed by a series of prehistoric tracks: straight-line roads he called ley lines, that were mapped out between important sites and marked by using or creating features in the landscape. Your prehistoric Briton, Watkins figured, took two locations of interest and then added to existing landscape features by building mounds and monuments in a straight line that anyone could easily follow. Signs of those tracks, he contended, are still out there. The locations of those trace monuments became sites of dwelling, safety and ritual, and persist today in place names, local legends and physical landscape features such as 'moats, mounds, camps and sites'. What's more, many of these sites came to be considered 'holy' by pagan locals and, in the Christian era, churches were constructed there.

The academy was skeptical. But a few decades later, Watkins' ideas found purchase with a rather different audience. Writer and paranormal researcher John Michell championed a hippie-friendly version of the theory. Watkins, he argued, was right about ley lines, but they weren't just prehistoric trackways. Michell and like-minded Earth mysteries researchers believed ley lines were related to earth energies that wrapped around the landscape. These lines had been understood by ancient peoples and had spiritual functions as well as practical ones, such as guiding UFOs around our territories. And more. A lot more. Energy dragons, Chinese astrology, numerology — anything and everything they could get their hands on. Ley lines came to represent to Michell and his readers physical proof of a once-great civilization whose knowledge has been eradicated by the introduction of modernity. These ideas merged with the counterculture of the period, and helped to make the landscapes around Glastonbury and Salisbury Plain (and Michell) an essential part of the late-hippie movement.

Michell's theories fit soundly within Simon and Mick's worldview. And isn't that always the case for the devout — that things *used to be* just fine? Conservative politicians, Blues aficionados, followers of trendy diets and the Old Testament alike — they all look back, whether to the 1950s, the Iron Age or Creation. In this case, Michell and Watkins, Simon and Mick, even dear old Hilaire Belloc, agreed that the 'thing' we had lost was still out there, hidden, waiting to be reclaimed.

I watched Mick, twirling his broom handle above his head, and Simon, conspicuous in camo against a grey suburban day, moving slowly around the church as though stalking some unseen prey. I wanted to believe, but it wasn't getting easier.

Coldean did have some ley line credentials. Watkins had believed 'col-' to be a place name associated with the 'cole man', the half-priest/half-engineer who sighted the leys. Perhaps this was 'the Downland valley of the ley-maker'. Simon assured me that St Mary Magdelene stood at a crossroad of ley lines, including a strong one that ran to a central power line on the South Downs.

But St Mary Magdelene came by its converted-barn decor honestly. I later found out that until the 1950s it had, indeed, been a barn. The ley-line principle was based on a site's antiquity — and I was struggling to find any signs of such a thing in Coldean. Mick fumbled and dropped his broom handle; I turned away as though I hadn't seen, wondering how long it would be before I could politely make my excuses.

But Simon made a grunt. His rods were turning.

"Come try this," he said to me, grinning. "I think I've found it."

I held the handles the way he showed me: lightly, like I was letting out a kite string. That film-noir gangster pose Simon had struck belied a Tai Chi looseness. It was harder than it looked; my instinct was to grip tightly, to either force or block some kind of movement from the rods. I walked counter-clockwise around the side of the church and my eyes drifted slightly closed. I too looked like I was stalking unseen prey. There was, it turned out, a method to it all.

"These churches were almost always built on ancient sites," said Mick, eyes closed, broom handle above head, a few feet from me. I stepped gingerly, trying not to jump the dowsing rods with my movement.

"More than likely, a well or a spring — water. You're approaching it now — those trellises on the church wall mark it."

I approached the spot Simon had found. I took a step into the space between the trellises. The rods, both held in front of me, turned to the right. I stopped; they stopped. I stepped; they turned. Simon's grin dug into the sides of his cheeks.

Long afterwards, while researching the history of the church, I opened Google Maps and used it to draw a dead-straight line between Whitehawk Camp, a Neolithic enclosure on the eastern outskirts of Brighton and the origin Simon cited for the ley line we sought, and the top of Ditchling Beacon, one of the highest (and, therefore, most sacred) points on the South Downs. There, exactly on the line and almost exactly halfway between the two sites, was St Mary Magdelene.

It had started to drizzle. The condensation was

dripping off the end of Mick's nose. I stood on the balls of my feet in the rain, rocking back and forth across the energy line, watching the rods.

The real people
Mick's cigarette smoke mixed with the rainwater-and-sweat condensation and the smog coming from Simon's hash pipe to form a dive-bar atmosphere inside the speeding car. We were careening up a country lane I could have sworn we had just departed. We were doubling back. I kept asking where we were going, peeking out from the back seat like a distracted toddler, but Mick would only say, "Happy Valley". Our journey was full of such conspiratorial precautions — code names, backtracks, circuitous routing. If only they had known just how lost I was, they wouldn't have bothered.

The last time I knew our location had been at Lodge Hill, a short stop we made between Coldean and our trip to the elusive Happy Valley. Lodge Hill is a short, flat embankment beneath the escarpment of the Downs. Archaeological evidence pins it down as a place of refuge in the Mesolithic and the Second World War alike, and legend cites it as the burial site for Dicul, the Saxon king who gave nearby Ditchling its name. It is a "holy hill", according to Mick.

As we walked from a nearby lane and onto the open-faced plain of the hill, a small stile leading to the land bore a sign declaring Lodge Hill PRIVATE PROPERTY. The owner allows the public right of way except for once each year, on 21st December, the winter solstice. That day, and only that day, the whole of the Hill is closed. But why?

I pointed to the sign with scrunched-up eyes. "Mick," I asked, "what could this mean?"

Mick continued with his "holy hill" spiel.

"There's no doubt that the *real people* used this site for communicating. Bonfires, smoke signals - something in my language."

My language, he kept saying. *Real* people. *Real* communication. Mick couldn't read and he couldn't write.

When I was at university, I had a roommate whose father couldn't read. He doted on his daughter, and visited frequently; once, early in our cohabitation, we all went to a meal at a family restaurant, and she read him the menu. I was confused. Eventually I came to face what was, in fact, fear — I saw this man's life, so unimaginably different from mine, as an existential threat. It took me most of the year we lived together to recognize my prejudice; to understand that education, or its absence, was a small aspect of his character. Just like Mick.

On Lodge Hill, I read the sign. Mick read the landscape.

"When the *real people* lived here, all of these plants, this holly, here, even that bracken on the side of the hill — it all meant something. Then the monks and the priests came. They took it all away."

Holly — fertility, strength, sustenance in winter. A heroic plant, hung in the house for comfort and security, its presence informed the *real people* that they were welcome in this place. Bracken — cut open a stalk and you'll find the initials of the ruler of the land upon which it grows, the *real* ruler, inscribed end-to-end like Brighton rock. Yew trees — they stand guard over churchyards and are entrances to the afterlife, signposts left to remind the clergy who is *really* in charge. It all told Mick the same thing: this is where you belong.

Sitting in a pub with Mick at the end of the day, I felt conspicuous reading the menu of bar snacks. It seemed insensitive to make notes with a pen and paper beside the open fire. Had Mick felt the same about me on Lodge

Hill, he the weary translator amidst an explosion of texts invisible to me? William Burroughs famously decried urban living's 'continual stream of second attention awareness. Every license plate, street sign, passing stranger is saying something to you.' I imagine that's what it's like for Mick as he strides up the Downs, a riot of language enveloping him, and so many of us passing by without noticing.

I was reminded of the way a similar scene was described by the 19th-century 'peasant poet' John Clare — another man born straddling two eras, two languages.

> … Each little tyrant with his little sign
> Shows where man claims earth glows no more divine
>
> On paths to freedom and to childhood dear
> A board sticks up to notice 'no road here' …
>
> As tho the very birds should learn to know
> When they go there they must no further go …
> And birds and trees and flowers without a name

Mick and I live in the same century, but our languages are as different as mine and Clare's: when Mick and I spoke, it was in unknown-unknowns. I can't read the field or the hill, but it's more than that. These words he used all the time — *real*, *connect*, *download* — I don't have them; not in the way he used them. So much of my world, of qwerty and silicon and hours at a desk, would be meaningless to Mick. More *un*real, more *dis*connected than Ascension Masters or calling on the rooks are to me. Mine is the world that puts up signs; Mick's is the world that ignores them.

Among the stones We parked the car at a lay-by on a small country lane, and ate pre-packaged corner-store sandwiches — slivers of cheese and an emaciated tomato on limp bread. Simon fetishized preparedness, and seemed reenergized by the austerity of the moment — pelting rain, awful food, the last muggy snorkel of his hash. I imagined his diary that night: 'We were somewhere around Balcombe on the edge of the forest when the drugs began to take hold...'

Simon pointed across the street to an old cottage with a garage full of tiny tractors, ATVs with a chip on their shoulders, to indicate that this was our direction. Impossibly, Simon managed to don *more* waterproofs, *more* camouflage, and he and Mick each drew a massive golf umbrella from the boot. Mick tucked his under one arm and stuffed a foot-long baguette into his jacket pocket.

"Do you have a staff," he asked, and handed over his spare — a waist-tall aluminum stick. I must have had a disdainful look in my eyes. "For walking," he said sternly.

Invisible from the street, a narrow footpath bordered the garage and tipped down the side of the hill beside a fenced-off piece of land. As we marched down the hillside I tried to picture our trio the way a passer-by might see us.

We looked ridiculous. Simon in two layers of camouflage, a huge pack on his back, a staff in one hand and golf umbrella in the other; me in soggy North Face jacket, scribbling furiously into a soaked notebook. Mick lagged behind. A few times I noticed him take covert bites of his sandwich, stuffing it into the side of his mouth, his front teeth either feeble or gone. It was the first time I appreciated how small Mick was and how gaunt, with wind-tanned skin pulled taut across his face.

After a quarter of a mile following the public right of way down into the valley, Simon glanced back at me and, without warning, put one hand on the fence and jumped over. Mick and I followed suit and, after a breathless jog into the underbrush, we crouched in pow-wow. Simon told me we should watch out for the gamekeeper.

"Gamekeeper?"

"Yeah, the gamekeeper," Simon said, though I understood it to mean groundskeeper. "He's usually out in the daytime. And he has a shotgun."

We stayed low to the ground, crouch-running, Navarone-style. It was exhilarating. We were leyline SAS. Perhaps the subterfuge was necessary — we were, after all, trespassing. Maybe it was another ploy meant to throw me off from discovering Happy Valley's true location. But whether by design or instinct, I think Simon and Mick were trying to make me see the landscape with a sense of wonder. The effect was intoxicating.

The valley we had entered was dripping with life — ferns and moss and a tree canopy high above that kept some of the rain out, yet occasionally dumped buckets on us. Every stone was slick, every step doughy. We skimmed through the ferns for a dozen meters or so, crouched low and keeping close, running silent and quick, when Simon suddenly stopped. In a single movement he stood straight up and opened his bright-green-and-white umbrella. It was all I could do not to slam into him, and Mick into me. I was still crouching, a patch of nettles biting through my thin trousers, when Simon said, louder than was strictly necessary, "Gamekeeper's passed. No shotgun." (I was sure there was no groundskeeper at all, but when we left later on I spotted him loading cleared brush onto a glorified golf cart.)

With the coast clear, we pushed forward, following Simon's umbrella. After a long, slow descent, the hillside leveled out. Simon closed his umbrella and used it to prise apart two leafy bushes, revealing the valley floor just beyond. We stepped into the open space and the rain ceased and the sun shone and the giant stones towered, indifferent to it all.

What looked at first to be the larger of the two formations was actually a pair of stones: a three-storey mass, tons of rock interlaced with veiny cracks and smooth bulbous mounts, sitting on top of another stone. The second, base stone, in contrast, was a man-sized wedge. It looked as though it had been temporarily slid underneath its gargantuan partner. This was Big-upon-Little, a balancing rock formation that might be famous were it not so well hidden and, ironically, so gargantuan. The big rock is so large as to overshadow its little perch and from some angles you can't see the pedestal at all. The overhang between the two rocks could shelter several brave adults from the elements, and has done for a long time: there is graffiti, blackened by fire, that attests to schoolboy visits during the 18th century.

The second formation Simon called the Druid Stone, slick pockets dug out of it on one side and a duct-like cut running straight down the middle. The cuts could be natural, the result of water erosion. But the locals who call it Executioner's Rock clearly don't think so.

Simon and Mick stood before the stones like the faithful, while I irreverently snapped photos, including one peering up along the Druid Stone's sluice. Simon told me that mine would be the only photo that existed of this site in all the world, and in that moment I believed him. He told me that if I climbed to the top, I would be one of only half a dozen or so people alive to have done so. This was Simon's greatest skill: to make a person experience the landscape with the thrill of a Victorian explorer, even if that landscape was only a mile from a mainline station. I climbed to the top, looked out upon those greens, those thorns, the vast ocean of a riotous natural world, emptied of human influence. A vision I knew to be an illusion.

Back on the valley floor, Mick and I went through

an arch-shaped stone to another part of the site that held
a large pond of clear water. The arch curved over one
end of the pond as well as its bank, such that one could
either walk through the entranceway, or launch a small
boat under it. At its opposite end the pond was hooded
in lily pads; trees ringed it almost entirely, their leaves
already beginning to phase towards orange, and there was
a further, distant rock outcrop. I had seen all of this from
the top of the Druid Stone, felt its tidal pull. I had wanted
to be subsumed, swallowed, by this landscape, and passing
through the archway felt like giving in to its maw. My
earlier anxiety receded.

    Mick, too, was different. He was sunnier. He sat on
a bald patch of ground, put his elbows behind him and
stretched out, cat-like; his eyes relaxed. He told me that
he had known this nook, and many like it, for decades.
Mick's mind, I imagined, held an index of such retreats
across the county, mapped out with shadows and paces.
He told me the pond was important to him because it had
been in a corner of the countryside just like this where, as
a child, Mick had first met them — the *real* people: Pan's
people.

Mick's enemy is real, but it is not the priests or the monks.

Mick grew up living and working on farms that, even by the time of his youth in the late 1950s, were practically feudal. His father was a cowman, the hand in charge of a large farm's cattle operations, and was renowned for being good at his job. He always had enough money to keep the family going, but he didn't bestow his son with much in the way of aspirations or opportunities. At one point in our smoke-filled dash across the Downs, we passed a small lane leading to a primary school. Mick slowed the car for a moment and we glanced up the lane.

"That's where I did my schooling. One day."

A single day in primary school constituted the entirety of Mick's formal education. He worked the farm with his family, and by the age of thirteen, he was on his own in the fields, driving a tractor.

"They paid me seven-and-six a week for being a good peasant."

For this wage, teenaged Mick would drive his tractor through the fields around Ardingly and Horsted Keynes. The tractor would record how far it had gone that day, so the farmer could check that its driver had done his share of the work.

"I rigged that tractor to go slow and straight without me touching it, and I'd lean back and sleep in the sun all afternoon, clocking up the hours."

Mick's world was the outdoors — the farmlands and woodlands and happy valleys around his father's workplaces. And there were many of those workplaces. Mick's father was prone to violent outbursts, and throughout his childhood the family was regularly disrupted when he'd fight with the farmer and have to move on. But he was good, and there was always another farm.

So began Mick's catalog of idyllic bolt holes around Sussex. In those times of trouble, he would seek shelter and solace by escaping to a hidden glen or high chalky Down. One day, as a young boy, he sat alone on a stone in the woods not too far from the farm his father was working — a site, he repeated, just like the stones we were sitting on beside the clear pond. A rustling in the brush disturbed him, and young Mick turned to see a small creature with an elongated face, pointy features, horns and a tail. It was, he said, no more than two feet tall. Later in life he recognized its likeness in Gothic gargoyles and cartoon devils. That was the first time Pan's people visited

Mick, a remnant of the *real people* that exists "to help us connect — to remind us that we *need* to connect".

A similar remnant crops up in the 1974 film *Penda's Fen*. A confused schoolboy wakes from a dream to discover an impish creature sitting on his chest — a kind of living gargoyle just like Mick's mysterious creature. A series of visions follows that calls into question the certainty of the staid world into which the schoolboy has been born: a fiery saint imploding both his faith and his sexuality; the ghost of Edward Elgar questioning his nationalism; eventually, his real-world mentors daring him to look further back, to find the cracks in the ideological certitude of conservative England. A vision of Penda — the last pagan king in England — gives the schoolboy an order:

> Night is falling. Your land and mine goes down into a darkness now; and I, and all the other guardians of her flame, are driven from our home, up out into the wolf's jaw. ... the flame is in your hands, we trust it to you: our sacred demon of ungovernableness ... be secret, child be strange: dark, true, impure and dissonant.

Long before *Penda's Fen*, Mick heard this same command and he followed it; he was secret and he was strange, and he was guarding a flame that appeared to have otherwise been all but extinguished. He guarded it across the hidden corners of the countryside that were, without question, *his* land. That flame is enchantment — the uncanny experience of the land that Whitman described: 'Something else is also here'. To Mick, the ability to join in that oceanic experience of the landscape — the mystic's experience of being subsumed by the view from a top of a stone, or the mirror stillness of a pond — is the most powerful kind of knowledge. It was his only defense from a difficult life, and it was the only one he needed.

Beside the pond, Mick was transformed. An hour before, he had been reserved and stumbling; by the stones and the water he became an extrovert. His father, Mick told me, was more than just argumentative. Sometimes he could be violent. Not only would he fight his boss, the farmer; sometimes he would even threaten the lord, as Mick still called the farm's landowner. Mick would have to learn new paths, new Downs, new hideouts. But despite his belligerence, Mick's father had also been a "people pleaser" — a phrase Mick spluttered like a curse.

"At Christmas, when the Lord gave me presents, my father would take them and give them away to other people's children - to get in good," says Mick.

He stood up and swept his arms, occupying space in a way I hadn't seen him do before, his arms swimming slowly from east to west and back again. He filled the valley.

"But what did I care? What did I want presents for? I had all this."

The field was our church Long after that day, I was reading John Clare again.

> I grew so much into the quiet love of nature's preserves that I was never easy but when I was in the fields passing my sabbaths and leisure with the shepherds & herdboys ... we heard the bells chime but the field was our church & we seemed to feel a religious poetry in our haunts

That was Mick. The field was his church, and his sermon was always the same — 'connection'.

"Life is hidden in the stones," he told me of the sarsens and standing stones that punctuate the English landscape. "People walk around the stones and are changed by them. Life is such chaos, but the stones give us a chance to connect — and if we can't connect, we can't disconnect; we've got to be able to let things go, to let people go."

The experience I had at the top of the Druid Stone: was that 'connection'? Mick's new-age buzzwords still troubled me; I couldn't quite give up my incredulity about something one can only know through experience. I wanted a ritual or a prescription, something to *do* in order to reach a goal.

I never saw Mick again, but a few years later I heard his echo. I had walked up a gentle incline outside Stanmer Park near Brighton and at its crest looked out over the rolling Downs to see, a mile away across the valley, a hillside poured red with poppies. There was, at that crest, an enclosure — a ring-fenced wood in the middle of a pathless cornfield that crunched underfoot. I circled around to the far side of the enclosure where Jess Bayley pointed me through a latch-gate and into the wood where two blue-hued sarsens lay half-exposed in the chalky earth. I had come to ask the stones for a sign, but they'd already given it.

Red with poppies

Jess had led me to the sarsen stones mindful of an exercise — one she asks regularly of course participants at the Centre for Ecotherapy, a not-for-profit organization she founded on a small plot of land on the Downs at Stanmer. "I ask people to consider something they're struggling with," she said, "and to go out into nature and ask for help in some way. To connect with nature in a way that allows it to reflect back to you; sometimes, to reflect back at you things about yourself that you're not even aware of."

Connect. Reflect. The stones, in which life is hidden.

Here I was back in Mick country, and here she was, speaking his language.

Wild is relative   I met Jess Bayley because I wanted to find out how Mick's ideas operated within a different vocabulary — one that existed in a world of accepted literacy and flourished in the academy, despite being rooted in the same square feet of chalky earth as Pan's people. Despite the courses she's taken, and now operates, and the university halls from which she holds certificates, Bayley's church is the field, her lectures given in birdsong. I could tell that the minute she leaned out of her rickety van to holler at me on the side of the road in Stanmer.

Jess is something of a punk pragmatist: the kind of woman who knows which mushrooms you can eat and how to fix a combustion engine. Her van smelt of caffeine and sweat like those of a thousand idealistic rockers, but with Crass-stickered tube amps traded in for tarps, bagged soil and strimmers. I thought she had picked me up in order to take me to the Centre for Ecotherapy office in the van, but it quickly became apparent they were one and the same.

If you picture the South Downs National Park as a river, Stanmer Park is an estuary: the tidal mouth at which the Downs and the rest of the world converge. Just off the A27 and bordered by the University of Sussex and Brighton's northern suburbs, Stanmer Park comprises an old manor house and pond, church and a tiny settlement with tearooms. It also boasts a large patchwork of green spaces run by organic artists and woodcrafters; a physic garden and the Earthship to which Mick and Simon considered bringing me; pathways canopied by trees; and acre upon acre of organic gardens. These were once the gardens of Stanmer House, the 18th-century seat of the aristocratic Pelham family. Later it became a nursery for Brighton, growing the flora for the city's parks and gardens. Now, it is run primarily by Stanmer Organics, a collective that has kept 17 acres of organic grounds for nearly two decades. (The Earthship — a self-sufficient, zero-emissions structure and one of the first of its kind in Britain — landed in 2006.)

The Centre for Ecotherapy turned out to be nothing more, or less, than two plots of this land: a large garden allotment and a 'wilderness' area. Jess walked me through the wilderness. The A27 is less than a mile away, not to mention St Mary Magdalene church and Coldean's semi-suburban houses. The University is a 15-minute walk across fields. And yet, in the Centre's small 'wilderness', none of this is visible or audible — there is the field, and there is birdsong; church and gospel. The Centre offers this downland peace to anyone who needs it, and in particular extends the green space to those who might have no other access to the natural world: the homeless, of whom Brighton has the second highest number in Britain, or those struggling with addiction or mental health problems.

"I know the healing power of nature," said Jess. "I reclaimed my own sanity by immersing myself in nature."

In her final year of university in Sheffield, Jess had a breakdown and, in a last-ditch effort to maintain her sanity, packed a rucksack and a tent and fled for Ireland.

While walking the wild Atlantic coast, Jess saw something reflected back at her that she'd never seen before. Playing her pennywhistle ("like a good hippie chick"), chatting at a campsite, striding along the cliffs — people saw something in her that she hadn't been aware of, and they liked it. A new confidence emerged when she looked back at herself from the glass of a stream, and she reemerged from the edge of madness.

She eventually returned to England, but Jess never went back indoors. She took any job that kept her outside, picking fruit up and down the country, sleeping in her van. She met her partner — they now have two teenaged sons - while picking hops in Herefordshire. One of them would ride in the 'crow's nest' of the tractor — a tube-enclosed ladder attached to the back of the vehicle — and cut the tops of the 14-foot-tall hop vines with a sickle. The rest of the crew would then lay the vines neatly in stacks on a flatbed. Change the method of locomotion, and the job would've been familiar to someone in 1900 or 1800.

Maybe that's the same with ecotherapy. Jess didn't need someone to tell her to get the hell out of the city and walk the countryside to reclaim her sanity. She did need Ireland — somewhere she saw, in her youth, as a magical landscape. Sometimes we need a push from the outside, something that unlocks our ability to see the landscape, and ourselves, in a new light. Ecotherapy is a set of such methods, essentially an umbrella term used to denote the marriage of contemporary therapies and wellbeing exercises to the outdoors. Skip the counselor's couch for a walk in the woods with your head-shrinker? Ecotherapy. Move your yoga class onto the Downs? Ecotherapy. Gardening for wellbeing? You're on it.

Jess and I walked the 'wilderness' to one corner of the grounds where a ring of tall posts was capped with the beginnings of a roof, a new permanent shelter around which to base the Centre's exercises. Each post hole was dug a meter deep, the land leveled, the posts sunk, all by volunteers, all by hand. The 'wilderness' is only about half an acre — but, bordered by nettles and coarse shrubs, and full of paths that spiral back onto themselves, it can feel far bigger. You could certainly get lost in it. 'Wild' is a relative term, and to many of those who use the Centre this *was* wilderness, far from city blocks. Some of the Centre's users come for active counseling, some simply to till the allotment or clear nettles from the wilderness.

"We humans are a *doing* creature," said Jess. "Quite a

lot of mental ill-health comes from and leads to a lack of activity; of purpose. Isolation. Outdoors, you can rectify those elements and swing them around by getting people involved. Somebody who's been unemployed or medicated for three or four years, in some cases half their lives, and they've never had the opportunity to do anything of practical value — get them working in the garden or up on a ladder building something, and it makes a difference."

There is a pair of elms at the heart of the Centre that Jess calls the "Yin-Yang Trees", two trees that have grown as mirrors of one another, their upper branches entwined. They are Jess's own avatars, the natural phenomenon in which she sees a reflection of her better self: growing side-by-side, completing one another. Beneath them, she tells me success stories — of the housebound or the homeless, or those struggling with addiction, whose lives have changed subtly but importantly through the simple act of working outdoors. An extraordinary one: a woman in her mid-fifties, coming from a situation of isolation due to depression. She'd been housebound for five years. She began coming weekly to work at the Centre and in three months began volunteering at an organization teaching literacy to adults — three months later still, this woman was doing the same thing as an employee, her first job in years.

"Working alongside others in the garden, she grew herself in a way that she not only came out of her shell, but felt able to give of herself to others."

Mick couldn't read. Jess had degrees. But they each employed the same language: the need to connect, to reflect, to attract; the realization of the self that occurs when we get to these points. Jess led me out of the wilderness and into the allotment, where beans and herbs and vegetables grow, all tended in biweekly sessions by those with little other access to anything green. She stood me over a staked-out pea patch, muddled thick with vegetable chaos. Stare into it, she instructed me, and find peas to pick — the fattest ones, not the young skinny ones; leave those. Just look until you've found the fattest pea pod you can, pick it, snap into it — they are so fresh, so ready, they crack like a percussion instrument. Eat.

"You're changing your eyes," said Jess. "You're focusing on this one thing, looking for this one thing, and doing that changes *everything*."

I was still looking for the right peas as Jess explained

a little bit about Attention Restoration Theory. The brain's capacity for focus, says the theory, is limited. We use it up quickly. To restore that attention we have to change our focus. Much of modern life requires what psychologists call 'directed attention' — tasks we concentrate on with effort. Nature offers us opportunities to focus on things that are less direct, less threatening, but which capture our attention — what's called 'soft fascinations', like passing clouds or a field of poppies or the line of a country path. Psychologists also note that a natural environment is restorative when it is immersive and away from everyday activities, and when the subject seeks the restoration — what they call compatibility.

I imagined Mick confronting these ideas. To him, and to many others, the requirements for generating compatibility in the person, and the soft fascinations that appeal to that person, might not be as simple as picking peas or digging postholes. To some, it's got to be something more grandiose: the unknown origins of a standing stone or a landscape carving in the chalk; an earth ritual or a ley line. But the result is the same — surrender to the landscape, and through that surrender, find comfort.

In the enclosure with the sarsen stones, I told Jess about Mick. I nervously relayed the uncanny connection between her words and his. I thought she might chafe at the idea that all her work and that of her colleagues in ecotherapy could be compared to an aged, illiterate wizard. This prejudice was mine, not hers.

"Every workshop I run I'm blown away by what people take from it for themselves, how they respond to a bird flying past or a dead tree with mushrooms growing from it," said Jess. "We are, gene-wise, part of nature; you can't have just 150 years of modernity and shrug off your genes. We're part of the land, part of everything around us — we've just forgotten it, or aren't encouraged to make something of it."

Yes, I said, that's what Mick might say — that we've lost something incredibly vital to our humanity.

"Not 'lost' — it's more finite. 'Mislaid', I'd say. 'Become unconnected to'. We were so much more in touch with the seasons, with what the birds or the trees are trying to tell us. That might sound crazy to some people, but if you hear a sudden squawking — those birds are telling you something, but we're not in touch with those parts of ourselves."

"Then again, many people are. Some of the people you've talked about, very much so. And they may seem very odd, but that's only because they're living *out there* a bit more than they're living in the modern world. Because they're connected."

VI CIRCLES

Trying to Believe at Cheesefoot Head

THE SOUTH DOWNS WAY BEGINS at an anonymous point above a field just east of the M3 motorway outside Winchester in Hampshire, along a winding path frequented by Lycra-clad joggers. There are signs for it earlier on, back towards Winchester, but the western extreme of the Way is about something quiet and we should let it begin where we feel it: at the point where the white noise of mechanization, of acceleration and shifting gears, begins to mix into the wind-hum of grass and squeak of starling. The road blends, too. Paving becomes stones, stones become stubble, stubble becomes soil and grass and, soon — before you know it, really, before you're actually ready for the town and suburbs to vanish — that grass becomes wheat.

I walked out of Winchester, hazy from a night at the Wykeham Arms with its free sausages, beautiful bartender and a clientele divided between 'students' and 'townies'. I had taken a perverse interest in watching two posh students drinking with a pair of lecturers. They bossed their elders, demanding they pay for more wine, and argued drunkenly about political scenarios they were too young to remember. I drank for an hour after I'd meant to leave just to watch these two smirk at everyone in the room — their elders, their peers, the bartender who rolled her eyes at their clumsy come-ons. And to watch the two men across the room who escaped their abuse: two middle-aged drunks arguing the merits of Tesco's own-brand wines. At one point I saw one of the students walk past them, almost into them; I imagined he might have walked right through them. "Did you feel something odd? A draft?" They existed in dimensions that barely touched.

The next morning I leapt out of bed, inhaled my host's homemade breakfast and hit the Way hard, trying to walk off the spin in my head. The first bit was easy: down a residential road and out onto a path, across a footbridge over the motorway, into the suburbs and pastures. But soon after, I was flummoxed by a diversion in the fields. The field was empty — harvested, or fallow — disguising what would otherwise be an obvious path across a farmer's land. Being hangover-hesitant, I chose to leave the marked path and go the long way around.

I'll never know exactly which route I took or in which field I saw, for the first time in my life, a vague series of shapes — a crude but unmistakable anomaly still visible in the corn's stubble. Three circles connected by a line, like a cartoon barbell but with a third circular 'weight' placed in the center. It was rough. But it was there: the ghostly remnant of that ultimate rural graffiti, the crop circle.

I stood and stared for several minutes as joggers passed by with a grunted '*pHey-ph*', a blur of neon and the faint waft of sunny-day sweat. It wasn't a great crop circle, not even a good one. But that's not the point. John Lundberg — one of the founders of an influential group of 1990s crop-circle makers — once told me that the first circle they had ever made was terrible: a single ring, and a poor one at that. But something remarkable had happened when it was discovered. News spread and believers started visiting. People felt nauseous just from standing in its center. Some had hallucinations; stories snowballed of the strange phenomena associated with the circle. Their botched experiment was taken up as part of the canon. People believed.

"For us, that was it," Lundberg said. "It wasn't about the physical act of making a circle, it was what that catalyzed. Something we felt was quite ridiculous had been elevated to the sublime — maybe even the divine."

I'd long hoped to see a crop circle. I wanted to be in on the joke. Here was my chance. I expected to feel a sense of superiority over the believers, secure in my knowledge of the circles' origins, and yet I stood there transfixed. The mistle-thrushes, squirrels, rabbits — just like the jogging passers-by, they never looked down. This was my first visit to Cheesefoot Head. I'd never seen the fields at Chilcomb Down and Matterley Basin and the Devil's Punchbowl. The circles, on the other hand, have been visiting for years.

Swirls of flattened wheat To the casual observer, crop circles began around 1980. In that decade and the next, they were everywhere — on newspaper front pages, every college kid's bedroom wall, on the lips of politicians and UFOlogists alike. But the circles had existed long before. Farmers in the Downs around Winchester remembered them from the 1950s, and there are even photos from before the Second World War. Respectable sources like the journal *Nature* and the Sussex Archaeological Society note the existence of crop circles as far back as 1880. And then there's a woodcut — a late-17th century piece that seems for all the world to show a circle formation being cut into a field of oats by a horned devil creature. But this we can say safely: the modern crop-circle *phenomenon* began at Cheesefoot Head in the late 1970s.

A mile north of Cheesefoot Head there once stood a

pub called the Percy Hobbs; it was there that two friends from Southampton occasionally met for a country pint. One evening, Doug Bower and Dave Chorley turned their conversation to 'UFO nests' — small crop circles that had appeared in the 1960s in Australia with no discernible origin. Doug and Dave discussed the possibility of the nests being manmade, which seemed a reasonable calculation, and decided to put the subject to rest. They returned to the Percy Hobbs the following week and, after their drinks, walked into a nearby field with a single implement — a steel bar — and began making an ever-widening circle of flattened wheat. Eventually their circle was 30 feet in diameter, the laid-down stalks covering the tracks they had left behind.

It was an inauspicious start — no one noticed, and even the duo could hardly remember the date. But it must have been fun, because Doug and Dave kept it up; more evenings at the pub and more circles appeared around Cheesefoot Head. Still no one noticed. By 1980, Doug and Dave had concocted a methodology and improved their technology. They used 'stalk-stompers', planks of wood attached to rope, to flatten the crops, and a monocle-like sight that dangled from the brim of a baseball cap to ensure the fidelity of their lines. They upped their game, increasing the complexity of their circles summer after summer. By 1981, the pair had expanded their operations to locations such as the Westbury White Horse, a famous figure carved into the chalk hillside on Salisbury Plain, where walkers might see their works.

Over the next ten years this mysterious artform flourished. The circles developed from simple rings and interlocking series of rings, to complex formations. Researchers began to visit the circles in search of answers. Scratch that: not in search of answers, but bearing them. Weather vortices and electromagnetic fields; experimental aircraft and UFOs; divine, occult and alien intervention. Each time someone came up with a new theory, Doug and Dave changed tack. By 1991, it was out of hand, and Doug and Dave had grown tired of the game. For reasons that remain their own, Doug and Dave hung up their stalk-stompers and made the rounds of the newspapers, outing themselves as the hoaxers who had been making crop circles for all these years.

Few took more interest than the young London-based

artists John Lundberg and Rod Dickinson, for they had recently turned their own attention to nocturnal circle-making. Like Doug and Dave, Lundberg and Dickinson wanted to test whether people *could* be behind the circles. That first, plain ring they made, which would be taken up by the community of believers, didn't provide many answers. "Even that was very difficult," said Lundberg. "After that first time, we were positive that aliens were involved."

Lundberg runs The Circlemakers — the squad that evolved around the work that he, Dickinson and a few others began. While artist and lecturer Dickinson has quit the game, Lundberg still makes crop circles, sometimes to order — if, for example, you're making a film that could use a formation. The Circlemakers are important to me not just because they made some of the most impressive and complex formations of the 1990s and 2000s, but because they did so with a clearly articulated philosophy. They considered their circles artworks, not merely because of the aesthetics of the formations, but because of the conversations and beliefs they catalyzed among believers. The circle was just the beginning. The stories people told, the lights they saw in the sky and the experiences they had in the fields — those narratives were the artwork. That process, however, relies on anonymity; a circle loses its potential if it is known to be manmade. So while Lundberg and his cohorts freely admit that they make crop circles, they'll never confirm which ones.

Lundberg calls the practice 'ostension' — a term borrowed from social anthropology, where it refers to real actions that play out folktale narratives. When the hallucinogenic or healing powers of an 'alien' crop circle are attributed to one of Lundberg's creations, the crop-circle narrative comes to life through ostension.

Mark Pilkington joined The Circlemakers after writing about them for *Fortean Times*, the house organ of the paranormal. On a trip into the fields with The Circlemakers, Pilkington stood in the middle of a crowded crop formation knowing that it hadn't been caused by weather anomalies or alien intervention or Celtic deities, but by the people standing right beside him. And yet there they were, dozens of people from around the world: some standing, some sitting or lying in the circle, meditating.

"In an old sense of the word, that was the most 'magical' thing that anyone I knew of could do. They were etching magical spaces into the landscape and the mundane laws of reality *changed* for people."

I left my perch at Cheesefoot Head and struck out east.
The route between Winchester and the village of Exton,
comprising many walkers' first full day on the South
Downs Way, is a relatively subtle one across Hampshire's
own chalk formation — the Winchester-East Meon
Anticline. If the Sussex Downs burst through the earth
in audacious *fortissimo*, the chalk folds of this anticline
tumble forth *poco forte*. Their geological splendor is spread
evenly rather than dolloped out.

Scrappy track-ways

The trail curved around crops and dog-legged
through tiny woods; it backtracked and swerved around
pasture and across A-roads. In Hampshire, the Way has
no obvious ridgeway to follow, so it's cobbled together
from a patchwork of scrappy trackways and walking
paths. I shared paved roads with cars, followed temporary
shortcuts, addendums and afterthoughts. You couldn't see
the Way unless you already knew it was there.

When I arrived in the village of Droxford, I was
midday-drowsy and sweaty with the previous night. I
ah-hemmed the landlord at the White Horse, tidying up
after the lunchtime crowd, and smiled for a pint. He was

new to command — the place was in transition, new beginnings in a structure that didn't care for such things. He and his staff — a single, slightly overwrought, middle-aged man — looked busy but distractable. I cast out a line: I'd seen a crop circle that morning.

The landlord had a scripted bartender's towel-over-the-shoulder friendliness, and he immediately took the bait: he knew the circles intimately. Before moving to Droxford, he had worked at the Barge Inn in Wiltshire — a famed hub of activity for crop-circle aficionados. Frequently, he said, there would be a gaggle of true believers swapping stories of a circle that had recently formed in the local landscape. Meanwhile, that circle's architect would be quietly sipping a pint beside them. We laughed, two skeptics, and the landlord told me that he'd be closing for the afternoon but that I should come back in the evening if I was still in the area. He poured me one more pint; and a shift beer for his employee, who pulled up beside me at the bar.

Game of enlightenment I'll call him the Actor. I could call him the Waiter, but he'd had speaking lines in a few episodes of *Midsomer Murders* and, according to the crew jacket he wore even on a hot day, he'd worked on a James Bond film. So who am I to judge? More importantly, he had faith. He knew something about crop circles, knew people who made them. And yet he believed.

When the pub closed, the Actor told me about the White Lion — it was open all day and served excellent ale, barely a mile's walk away. Why don't we just head out for an afternoon pint? His gambit had the practised self-deception of the daytime drinker. Behind the local church and beside the river Meon are the remnants of the Meon Valley Line, one of the spindly downland railway lines that closed in the 1960s, turning towns into villages, villages into hamlets and abandoned tracks into rural pub-crawls. We soon came across a tumbling-down wooden sign that announced we were entering Soberton. Its name would swiftly be proven untrue.

At the pub, the Actor told me how tough it was being a "background actor" (read: *extra*). There was a real artistry to it, he said, and *Midsomer Murders* was a perfect playground. A tongue-in-cheek TV detective show about eccentric rural crime, *Midsomer* is, in essence, 'about' the landscape in which it is shot — the places and the people that comprise the background. The story is just a spectacular lens through which you see the beauty and flaws of the setting.

"It's like crop circles," he said, though it seemed like a non sequitur. He'd sat by, mostly out of the fray, during my brief conversations in Droxford. But it had got under his skin and now he was ready to help me see the other side.

"People make crop circles, of course they do. But that's not all there is. *It's just not enough.* What if there's something else? Well, there is. There *is* something else, behind the scenes."

I didn't understand what he meant until long afterwards, when I met former Circlemaker, Dr Rob Irving. Irving is the intense and academic one — he even wrote his doctoral thesis on the topic. According to his research, when a crop circle is combined with a landscape's narrative — its legends, its history, its archaeology — the circle can lend a new perspective to that landscape. So when a circle appears in a place like Cheesefoot Head, with its decades of circle lore, or the 'legend landscapes' of Wiltshire around Stonehenge, Avebury and Silbury Hill, something powerful happens.

"You're connecting to that system" of landscape,

memory and myth, said Irving. "You're making this connection to the same views our ancestors had." And yet you never would have stood there, never would have looked outwards with that perspective, until that circle appeared. The circle makes the place, and everything that surrounds it, special. "If you put a circle out in the middle of a field, even just a simple circle, the people that are in it are thinking that just by being there, they are in some way special. It's a separation from all the people who just drive along the road and don't bother to go there. "There's a game going on. A game of enlightenment."

It wasn't long before I was walking out of Winchester once again, trying to retrace my steps out of the east of the city and onto the footbridge that crossed the motorway. It was a busy morning — my hand ran along suburban hedges bordering the South Downs Way, and I could hear children running and shouting on the other side. Soon afterwards, there were gunshots from a nearby army range. This time, I could see where the path was, but ignored it and continued on the route I thought I had taken before.

I hardly noticed when I reached that point — the point where the Way truly begins; where the starling and

Etched into earth

mistle-thrush takes over from the playground and the rifle range. There was another jogger, which seemed like a good sign — this was their territory. The lycra flash cued a sense memory, and I realized that I could no longer hear the cars from the motorway over the sound of the breeze amusing the just-yellowing leaves. It seemed right, seemed to be the same place I'd been before, but the plough had been and the turned earth bore no sign of the circles.

The air was crispening. There was activity all around — new lines being drawn in the fields. There would be hay bales on the way to Corhampton, north of Droxford; stacks of gold in rows. And in the field that dipped below me near Cheesefoot Head, the black dirt was churned with straw, straight marks etched into the earth.

VII RUINS

A Ghost Walk through Deserted Balsdean

MIXED IN AMONG THE CHALKS and flints that were lined up like toy soldiers along the branches of a felled tree were sheep's vertebrae — nearly a spine's worth. And tiny lamb's leg bones, blanched by the sun and polished by months of evening rain. Sanitized by the elements, any sinewy roughness or discoloration rinsed away, the bones looked ready for sale. You could string them around your neck, or stick napkins through them on the dinner table.

The first time I had visited this place I'd found a cow's skull lying on top of a half-buried stone — all that remains to mark the site of a thousand-year-old church. A sudden chill had sparked when I strode up the roll in the field and spotted the skull, bright white like a trophy, shining in the grass.

This time, there they were: sheep's vertebrae. And there it was: that chill. In a way, that chill *is* Balsdean; all that remains of what once was a bustling farm and Georgian hamlet, and a medieval village before that. Today there are no inhabitants, almost no buildings, and hardly a sign of the ones that once were. There is no dot on the map. Few people could point to it or give you directions. There is only that chill — the valley-wind, which seems not to tickle the grass or the leaves yet whips against your face — and the prodigious mist, only just beginning to burn off in the morning sun.

'Deserted Balsdean, a 'wisht' place,' is how it was described in the early 20th century. 'It has about it an eerie feel'. It is a place in which we sense the gaze of an unseen watcher: 'wisht' — meaning not just 'hushed', as in quiet and ghostly, but implying that 'something unseen is also here'; a place that's watching.

I stopped to rearrange my outerwear against the wind and a church bell struck nine. I didn't hear the bell from the north or from the east. It came from all around, the way your pulse and breath reverberate when you're in silence or cold — the dene-sound of the bowl-like valley. Balsdean's deception: the sound of every voice, every whinny and neigh, every twittering bird and foot-falling runner above me on the Downs seemed to come from everywhere and yet to come from nowhere.

Ethereal remains

The first time I had come to Balsdean it was not of my doing. I had asked to be brought to the site of 'the last home on the Downs', as Robert had described it — Robert of Peacehaven. We had ventured out from the suburb and walked a long road through innumerable hills and valleys before arriving at Balsdean and the cow's skull. There was a building — a barn — that stood next to the foundation of what had been a farmhouse, destroyed, I was told, by artillery practice leading up to D-Day.

This is why I had returned: if downland life had once existed in Balsdean in a manner that no longer exists anywhere, then surely there are traces? There are physical scars at Balsdean — outlines imprinted on the landscape. But Balsdean's ethereal remains can be just as potent: memories that ambush you as a sound on the wind, a glance over the shoulder.

I heard the church bells, the echoing footsteps from miles away, and now a voice. A woman's voice in my head — an older woman who seemed to be speaking only to me and only of this invisible place that I sought in the mist and the chill.

Of the two primary types of valley in downland place-naming, *-denu (-dene, -dean)* is, ostensibly, the less dramatic. Valleys the Saxons named *-cumb (-combe, -coombe,* etc) are sublime features, steep thumbprints stamped into the earth. Denes, on the other hand, are dendritic courses of ancient waterways now long-dried,

Back-stage in Bals-dean

forming nooks and crannies as well as wide valleys, all of which exist at Balsdean. They are easier to hide, and easier to hide in, despite sometimes being wide enough to hold a farm.

Balsdean is a dene such as this: long and flat at its bottom, coursed with pathways at its pinched ends and surrounded by high downs that shelter it from prying eyes. The valley is only a mile and a half from the residential neighborhood of Woodingdean, floating in the pool of green map that separates Brighton & Hove from Lewes and their seaside suburbs. The hills around Balsdean are covered with paths favored by runners, dog walkers and OS Map explorers — there is almost always someone up there. Yet on my walks through Balsdean itself I have never encountered another person. Even when I could hear people talking or working on the hills, could almost hear them breathing. In Balsdean I was dislocated, as though the performance of my own life was going on elsewhere and I was backstage, catching only vague signals and cues from just beyond the crest of the Downs.

Today, Balsdean exists in its valley only as a series of absences. The village doesn't appear to you as you enter, it recedes *away from* you. Remains identified from a distance disappear as you draw closer. I wended around the Norton Road as it descended from the level top of the downs and into the valley and saw ridges cut into the sides of the hills — waves, like a corrugated rooftop placed on a slant and covered in grass. It's a trace of the farming technique medieval residents used to extract some kind of economy out of this undulating land. But as I drew closer, the ridges became invisible, like slats on a Venetian blind. At the point where the ground flattened into the dene floor, the path crossed another leading up the hillside on the northern side of the valley. Just past the crossroads, I noticed the shapes into which these paths divide the land — like blocks of dwellings. Out of the corner of my eye, I thought I saw a structure. I turned my head to see nothing but a few modern foundation stones poking from the ground.

I scoured the long grass to the side of the path, searching for something tangible; a presence, rather than an absence. The stone on which I once found the cow's skull, far enough off the path to defy passers-by and even some who seek it. Drilled into the half-buried stone was a small plaque that marks 'the site of the altar of the Norman

Site of the altar

church of Balsdean'. I could almost catch the chapel's presence, draw its floorplan in my mind's eye, but then it, too, was gone — replaced by the chill of the wind.

Balsdean once consisted of two large farms and a tiny, thatched Norman church serving them. The hamlet thrived in some form from at least the 11th century until some time in the 18th. By the time James Watt finished his steam engine, the little thatched chapel was being used as a stable, and it was a place that passing walkers already considered eerie.

Even after the community scattered, a farm still stood there. In 1825 a license was granted to transform part of that farm into a paupers' lunatic asylum. The name 'Balsdean' came to be associated with that darker purpose. Sussex men admonished their rivals by declaring them 'Better fitted to inhabit the house at Balsdean than to assist a lame dog over a stile' and by saying that those who had come to their senses must have 'received the benefit of the skill of certain professional Gentlemen at Balsdean.' The chapel stood for more than five hundred years; the asylum didn't last five. By 1829, the patients were transferred up the road to Ringmer, northeast of Lewes. Yet the asylum left an indelible mark on Balsdean. A century after its dissolution, in the decade before the Second World War, the Rottingdean folk singer and author Bob Copper recalled seeing padded rooms still intact on the upper floors of the abandoned farm.

The War would be the final undoing for dwelling in Balsdean. In 1942, the farm buildings were taken over by Allied soldiers who used them for target practice. They were the last of its full-time inhabitants, ending a chain of settlement going back to at least the Norman invasion.

'Follow the valley past deserted Balsdean, a 'wisht' place amongst whose wildflowers lurks a vague flavour of ghosts,' wrote archaeologist and antiquarian A. Hadrian Allcroft in 1922. 'They have left their handiwork in what is called Kingston Castle on the hill-top to the west, and in a net-work of banks and ditches that wander aimlessly up and down the valley's sides.'

Before entering the footprint of the abandoned village, I descended through strata of sheep, the only cizitens of Balsdean today. The first time I'd visited, it was in search of something tangible — a structure, something of substance both physical and historical; something you could put a pin in. I'd come back looking for something less corporeal — a chill, a sound, nothing more — and yet it felt, if anything, *more* real. I was looking for a memory in the landscape, and here it was, all around me — not post-holes or chalk carvings but the mere lick of the wind. All I needed was the right guide.

Exactly where it was

The voice in my head was one of those ghosts. But the voice in my head was real. 'Nineteen forty-six. During, you know, rationing times. I can tell you exactly where it was...'

I heard this while passing a cement foundation poking through the grass in grey patches, like Lego studs protruding from the green. The ghosts had led me down this path, promising hints and traces, and here they were: the cement foundations of farm buildings emanating from the earth beneath a barren tree, hillsides terraced with steppes and mist, the plaque-embedded stone. Just beyond, a roofless barn bore graffiti in thin red paint: 'Lewis James Ewan *Will Die*'.

The voice was from an audio piece called '1946' by the Brighton-based duo Grasscut. It lies at the heart of their album *1 Inch / ½ Mile*, a record designed to be listened to on a walk through Balsdean, with landmarks signaling each piece's starting point in a poetic mapping of the valley. Broken-down and rusting machinery, the gate at the end of the path, even the mist-gauzed view from the top of the Downs: each corresponds to a part of the work. 'I can tell you exactly where it was...' This was a recording of composer Andrew Phillips' mother discussing her childhood, but I heard it while scanning the slopes for the plaque-stone, a tap on the shoulder in a deserted landscape.

Coming down through the mist into the valley I heard creaks of rusted metal, cello, piano, and another voice — 'so I walked and I walked' — and I passed through the gate. Describing the kind of air I cut through that day, the poet Jen Hadfield has used the Shetlanders' word for a thick, gauze-like fog, 'Stumba'. She writes of an air in which 'gates hang on hinges of fog'. This is the feeling of listening to Grasscut at Balsdean: a gate hanging on hinges of mist. Once opened, once passed through, we're backstage, behind the landscape, mingling with those disembodied sounds and memories.

The receding parts of the village, little mementos of loss, were illuminated by this musical accompaniment, and the farmhouses seemed to materialize into view. The roof on the barn: I could suddenly imagine it replaced.

Those sounds of work, real sounds of tractors and horses above on the downs, reverberated as though they were beside me, within the valley. A boy and a girl were standing beneath the tree, either side of the gate, each passing a ring over it to the other. Joining the creaks on my ghost-soundtrack was the crackle of shellac and the Irish tenor John McCormack singing, 'When life is o'er / When I no more can think of thee / When I shall be at rest upon my bed of roses…' 90 years of record-dust included.

> *Still on my lifeless hand, may it rest tenderly*
> *this little silver ring that once you gave to me*

To maintain the sublime In the early 20th century, the poet A. Stanley Cooke visited the site and there he found, in 'The Ruined Norman Chapel at Balsdean', 'some memory of its care for holy things'. His imagining of Balsdean still resonates:

> *Lost 'mong the hills — yet found of him who seeks —*
> *Roofless and gaunt it stands,*
> *Its graveyard nettle-choked. Tho' mute it speaks*
> *Of long-neglecting hand;*

Of hearts estranged; of deadened souls of men
Content to see but a cattle pen.

Walking out of Balsdean there is a doorway of sorts — a narrow pathway between the Downs leading to the next valley. It's there that I found the sheep's bones, carefully placed on a tree branch, above stones and pebbles that were once farm workers' homes. Foregoing that pathway, I began to climb the steep side of the Downs and as I did so, turned to peer back, watching as the scene below receded into distance and weather.

Tools discarded by a fence builder on the hillside appeared to have been there for months, even years. In that valley of loss, each pebble was as a vessel storing the memory of a home and of all the people that had once lived within. Once I had trespassed through the hinges of mist, every object appeared imbued with a life's story; a mine of memory awaiting my scouring hands.

On the final track of their Balsdean sequence, to be listened to on the ascent out of the valley, Grasscut includes samples of poet Ezra Pound reading from 'Hugh Selwyn Mauberly' and Hilaire Belloc singing 'The Winged Horse'. Both men were caught between England and another home; both disillusioned with life and history. And in the works that Grasscut has chosen, these writers imagine themselves as they levitate above England and modernity. They look down and watch as the nation and the present-tense recede into obscurity. 'The age demanded an image of its accelerated grimace.' Pound's voice haunted me as I climbed out, back into the world of electricity pylons and dog walkers.

The piece ends with Belloc singing a single phrase, layered over itself dozens of times so as to become a terraced wash of voices, seeming to come from everywhere and yet from nowhere.

And I ride, and I ride...

Balsdean exists below, but I cannot tell you exactly where it was.

VIII SEARCHING FOR DORIS

Part Two

THE DAY THAT PHOTOGRAPH WAS TAKEN was so happy. It was the garden in Surrey, far away from the traffic and the madness of London. She loved those few square-yards of earth that she and Bob — yes, even Bob — tilled and watered and scaffolded with branches for the climbers; scattered its tiny paths with stones. The garden faced south, caught the sun, and didn't Bob look handsome with his suit and pipe?

They were dressed for a rare night out on the town — exciting, though she didn't like to leave baby John, she doted on him so. But she loved to get dressed up and do her hair properly, waved off to the side like Norah Baring, rather than the make-do center-parting she wore when the little one was pulling at it. And that dress — her little black dress. It wasn't as little as some might wear, but it was perfect for her. She wore her wristwatch as her only jewelry, and a belt studded with buttons that she let dangle at her side, like you did. No makeup, black pumps — you can't have everything, Bob — but, sleepy new-mum eyes or not, didn't she just look gorgeous, so?

And Bob, his slim frame squeezed upwards to shuffle himself into the pebbly path though he didn't really fit beside her, his hair beeswaxed upwards a flip. The bank got more of his time than seemed right, but she didn't mind sharing because Bob was home each evening and making good on his promises to take care of them both, no matter what happened with John. John, whom she couldn't yet imagine as more than a rambunctious toddler, a joyful nuisance. But then again there were all the things that the doctors had said. Wasn't it a sunny, happy day, just?

It was nice to have a portrait made with only the two of them, together, ready for the world — one where she didn't have her hip cocked out to balance John or, worse still, her chin pulled back to check on his swaddled majesty. Bob always looked good — she thought maybe he cared a bit too much, but she wouldn't mention it.

She was a bit worried, but it was still such a happy day. She knew something was coming — it hadn't been easy, and it wasn't going to get easier. It wasn't even that it would get more difficult, just that it might never be less so. The other children would grow and fend for themselves. John, perhaps not. There was a sadness behind her heavy lids, but no hesitation in her smile. She had Bob, she had John, each one in sickness and each one in health, forever, no matter what. No matter what.

She was frightened, but that was normal and it was

still such a happy day. There was a risk, always, with a child like John, and it loomed in the back of her mind, but she had already learned to plaster over it. And, yes, perhaps it was more of a risk than she sometimes let on. Perhaps it was as high as fifty-fifty — they didn't always see it through, children like John, but she was only a little bit frightened; it's just that she was a little bit frightened all the time. Nervous. That love was frightening — the unconditional love coupled with this knowledge, all of these unknowns; more so than the other mums, the ones whose children didn't have anything different and what would they all say? The mums, the children? But her family, and Bob's, too, they didn't care. Sometimes there was a sideways glance. They didn't care. They were happy.

John was two, such a funny age, and everyone loved him and laughed with him (with!). Had there ever been a more loved child? They all think that, she was sure of it, mums; and yet it was also true — there hadn't been, not ever. Two was a wonderful age for John, a relief; three would be better still. And if he made it to three he'd more likely than not make it to four. And if not — her wrist, she should turn it out to face the camera so that the watch Bob gave her showed. It was so gorgeous and, if she said so herself, more than a little bit fancy. He was rising in the ranks at the bank. Come to think of it, maybe she'd work again herself — she'd had a job as a secretary, and she liked working in London. Croydon was peaceful and not far from the city on the train, but it was a different world from the bustle of her growing-up years, with Father until, but she couldn't even remember that, could hardly remember him at all, Father; and then with Mister Greenin, who had been just as much of a father, though now he wasn't well either but — maybe she could work again? She wouldn't get her hopes up. Who knew what would happen with John, and he was what mattered most. Maybe, she imagined, they'd move the other way, further out from London, somewhere with a few more miles in between and a bit more sun. Southend, Brighton or Eastbourne; somewhere beside the lovely sea? Because it's not far but maybe it's too far and —

— Smile.

IX LEVITATIONS

Listening to the Bells at Chanctonbury Ring

IT WAS THE FIRST OF MAY and I was up long before the day began. There was a half-inch layer of mist covering everything. The spider's webs, the Stella empties, my breath — all were coated with a milky film and a floral taste like fresh-cut herbs. The mist was thick enough for a garbage truck to miss me on the narrow side street I'd ducked down to cut through the park. I jumped out of the truck's path in a lopsided pirouette, heart in throat, and was suddenly reminded that I had learned this cut-through thanks to a funeral. My family picnicked in that park the day after my grandmother was lain to rest, the last time we would all gather in Steyning. Even in those twitterns and lanes, the seasons cycle around and around.

On the Round Hill at the outskirts of town, in the rising sun's dull glow, the dawn-choristers flocked up the Downs and it wasn't long before I could see Chanctonbury Ring in the distance. The ring of trees seemed to levitate between earth and sky, battered and broken as though its spine was snapped. As I've done for 30 years since the storm, I repopulated the shattered ring in my mind with ghost trees, envisioning its full complement of beeches, a flourishing island in the stark ocean of the Downs. Some of the dots on the horizon, within the Ring, were moving.

When I approached the Ring I could see that sheep had clustered inside. They were corralling their lambs among the standing and felled trees. In the center, the mist hugged the outline of the ancient hill fort. Wisps of wool snagged on the nearly barren spring branches, dressing the trees like dream-catchers, each one a memory, and I thought of Belloc.

> The moon stood over Chanctonbury, so removed and cold in her silver that you might almost have thought her careless of the follies of men ... Sleep came at last to me also; but that night dead friends visited me in dreams.

I walked onto the mound of Chanctonbury Ring and heard the sound of bells coming from the swaddling mist. If there is a 'thin place' on my personal map, it is Chanctonbury, where a glimpse of another world peeks through. I fell into a haze, like the warm befuddlement of cold-medicine. I imagine that believing in something, truly and deeply believing, sometimes feels a bit like this: buzzed with a warm confusion. That morning, I heard bells ring out in the mist and saw, levitating just barely above a fallen tree, my grandmother's ghost. The briefest flash in the corner of my eye, and then she was gone.

At its fullest extent, the ring of trees on top of Chanctonbury Down was thick enough to harbor darkness at midday. But the site was famous long before the trees. Chanklebury, Changebury; Chanctonbury: that name rang out like a bell in the mist for 2,000 years before the trees were planted. The Saxons found ruins at Chanctonbury when they arrived in Sussex, and invented myths to explain them.

The archaeological evidence suggests the hilltop was used for ritual purposes as long ago as the 8th century BC — rumors persist that it was used by the Druids for animal, and possibly human, sacrifice. The Romans recognized its holiness and built two temples on the site. Even today, a group of Christian churches around its northern side use it as their totem, occasionally venturing onto the hillside for outdoor worship.

Little is known about the site's history in the intervening centuries. Sussex historian Janet Pennington cites a curious incident from the 14th century in which a monk was killed at Chanctonbury on the 'eve of the Nativity of St John the Baptist'. This was a night marked in the medieval period by the lighting of bonfires and raucous celebrations, which takes place on 23rd June —

the summer solstice.

Was this incident isolated? 'The traditional meeting-place of Sussex witches is Chanctonbury Ring,' writes Doreen Valiente in *Where Witchcraft Lives*. Her implication is that the witches' coven that meets at Chanctonbury represents an unbroken line of ritual practice stretching back to the old paganism of ancient Sussex. The coven is almost certainly a figment of Valiente's vigorous imagination. But the sentiment of a place of ritual — of life and death — was there.

The ring of trees dates to 1760. The heir to the nearby Wiston estate was a teenaged boy named Charles Goring; his descendants still run Wiston and tend to Chanctonbury. Charles had fallen in love with his family's landscape and this Down in particular, crowned as it was by an Iron Age hill fort — a ring of trenches and earthworks from the time before Christ. But rather than follow the antiquarian urge to dig for knowledge or plunder, Goring celebrated this place by planting trees around the rings of the earthworks. Throughout his long life he tended to these trees, watching them become an icon of his beloved Downs.

That May morning, I walked the circumference of the Ring, now thinned by the Great Storm of 1987. I had come to scour the Ring for a fallen tree trunk — the place I had sat as a child, a brief moment alone, on my first visit to Chanctonbury — and I was looking for some sign, some clue, as to which route to take through the stubborn earthworks and knotty undergrowth; some kind of reminder to stretch my memory back nearly 30 years. But there was something else to attend to first: those bells.

They were faint, muffled by the mist, but they were definitely real. Too thin to be the clang of a half-broken stile, too high to be the gong of an animal's collar. They belonged to someone, and that someone was watching.

The poet John Masefield describes this feeling of being watched on the Downs:

> Up on the down the red-eyed kestrels hover
> Eyeing the grass.
> The field mouse flits like a shadow into cover
> As their shadows pass.
>
> Men are burning the gorse on the down's shoulder,
> A drift of smoke
> Glitters with fire and hangs, and the skies smoulder
> And the lungs choke.

Once the tribe did thus on the downs, on these downs, burning
Men in the frame,
Crying to the gods of the downs till their brains were turning
And the gods came.

And to-day on the downs, in the wind, the hawks, the grasses,
In blood and air,
Something passes me and cries as it passes,
On the chalk downland bare.

Danc-
ing
in the
May The bells were growing louder. Voices, too. There was an
unseen watcher, and it was me.

I circled back to the other side of the Ring to see
straw hats ringed with flowers emerging from behind the
hillocks, bobbing at the edge of Chanctonbury's fortress.
I hung back, biding my time until a critical mass had
arrived at the eastern edge. They were dressed in the
traditional garb of the English folk dancer — all-white
with bright red sashes, bells sewn into their boots and
trousers, hats and vests studded with buttons and spiked
with feathers: the Chanctonbury Morris Men.

They were at the Ring to 'dance in the May' — to
welcome the month favored by English poetry and folk
song. The Morris men were leaning against the trees,

obsessively straightening sashes and adjusting bells. There were more of them than us bystanders. Other than myself, I counted a few partners and wives, two German tourists and a freelance photographer whose shots would eventually grace a few of the regional papers. It was misty, raining, chilly, very early in the morning, and almost no one was watching. By earthly standards it was not a great gig.

The men began to dance.

They lined up facing each other at the outer edge of the Ring, two rows of dancers, and hopped, turned, kicked and clashed sticks to a mild concertina tune. Morris dancing is militant. The men begin like a battle-ready unit, arms stiff at their sides, before sliding together and apart like a line dance. But rather than drag feet across the floor or *do-si-do*, they crack their wooden sticks together in faux-swordplay, tapping their sticks on the ground as if to egg on their opponents, and raising their arms in victory.

Morris dancing won't make the rains come; nor will it enrich the harvest. It is a checkpoint, a diary entry written into the earth with footsteps, like lines accrued on a face. That is the purpose of tradition: to be enacted over and over again.

As the dance continued, I backed off into the trees, searching. On the northwest side of the Ring something sparked a familiar feeling — the snap of a twig underfoot, the skid of a dew-slickened patch — and I took it as a sign. I moved closer to the center of the trees, many of which were small, newly planted, spring-budding. There, among the snagged wool and mist, I stepped over a lump in the ground. I spun around, one hand on a young tree to steady myself, and there she was. Winnie.

Tales
like
spells I don't often see the dead. Certainly no more than anyone else, because we *all* see the dead, don't we? Waiting on a cloud-darkened bench, or passing by us on a side-street, or fumbling for their keys in the hallway?

She was sitting on a section of tree prone on the ground - not not on, above it. Maybe only half an inch, but she was above it, hovering, a fuzz of air between her body and the wood. I might not have recognized her but for the clothes: a utilitarian walker's skirt, tennis shows, a thin beige windbreaker. Her hair showed the first sparks of its corona of grey. Her elbows were pinned back, as if she was holding a teacup and saucer. Winnie Hopper, my dead grandmother, just as I remembered her from my childhood walks. She didn't move or make a sound, and when I turned my eyes directly towards her, she was gone.

In October 1987, Winnie hunkered down in her home beside the park in Steyning, at the foot of the Downs east of Chanctonbury. Outside, the Great Storm ravaged the land. Other than her dog, Polly, she was alone. It wasn't supposed to happen — the weather forecast had predicted heavy rains, but had said little of the wind. The South Downs are used to strong winds — the stubborn gorse and thick-ankled livestock is shaped by it; and Winnie's face bore its reddening whip. But nothing was ready for this.

Outside Steyning, the wind surpassed 100 miles per hour, churned and buffeted for hours at a time, and whittled away at everything from trees to houses to electricity pylons. On the phone a few days later — when it became an option, once again, to speak to Sussex — the first thing Winnie choked to us was that 'dear old Chanctonbury' was gone.

She would not have hidden — would not have given the storm such satisfaction. More likely she sat in my grandfather's armchair, Polly on her lap, the upholstered wooden back of the chair turned to the window in case it didn't hold. Her husband, my grandfather, had died four years before; his ashes were interred in the churchyard a block away. She was 16 years younger than him, he already a widower when they met.

On one of my first trips to England, Winnie took me for a walk to Chanctonbury Ring. By then she had already lived in Steyning for 20 years. She had little patience for my stubby child's legs and seemed not to understand what a trek this was — when I returned to school that September, I boastfully asked my American friends, "What's the farthest you've ever walked?"

We passed through the hollow-way of Mouse Lane, a road in use for at least 500 years under that name. It cuts through the landscape like an incision, walls of root-riddled earth towering on either side. We turned onto the Downs, climbing through tree-covered hillside, the canopy hiding the views from us until we emerged at the crest and looked out on the Ring and the South Downs Way spiraling beyond. Even as a child I could feel that Winnie became someone else when she walked. Normally she was both pragmatist and pessimist: she believed strongly in avoiding the embarrassment of failure rather than embracing the possibility of success. But out on the Downs I knew another Winnie — one who guided me along pathways and told me tales like magic spells.

As we walked, she told me about Chanctonbury's origins. It was, she said, all because of the Devil's Dyke. Just a few miles east of Chanctonbury, the Dyke is a deep, dry *coombe* cut into the landscape by a river created by the melting Ice Age permafrost. The river is gone, but the spectacular valley remains. That's what really happened, but Winnie's story was better.

The Devil, she said, wished to destroy Sussex. (In folk legend, the Devil was always itching to destroy Sussex for any number of reasons.) So off he set to wander that infuriating county and muse on its fate. Fire — the Arun and Adur and Ouse ablaze, unholy blue flame licking at Arundel castle and the thatched roofs of Steyning? Or earthquake — the cliffs crumbling onto Lewes; Winchelsea and Rye cut loose to the sea? He encountered a wise old woman and, being a cocky fellow, Beelzebub gave her the choice of how her homeland would be destroyed.

Flood, she said; that's the appropriate ruin for England's coast — but how to do it? After all, the Downs shelter Sussex from the sea. To cut through the hills would take ages, the wise woman prodded, even for the likes of the Devil. The bait was taken, and the bet was made: he would cut through before the cock crowed daybreak, or the Devil would leave Sussex alone. Satan dug and cut through the night and would've succeeded, but before he could, the old woman carried her lantern over the hill, fooling the cockerels into thinking day had broken — they crowed and Sussex was saved. But before he was stopped, the Devil furiously shoveled mounds of chalky earth to and fro. The earth landed across the county, becoming Mount Caburn, Rackham Mount, Ditchling Beacon, Cissbury Ring and, of course, Chanctonbury.

There are many versions — Belloc has St Dunstan instead of an anonymous woman, and prayer rather than guile. But the Devil is always there. Winnie continued with him as we approached Chanctonbury Ring. She told me that running around the ring seven times "widdershins" (counterclockwise) would summon him. That story changes, too, the summoned becoming in some tellings a legion of Roman soldiers or a horde of Saxon warriors, a twinkling of faeries, a murder of crows or a clattering of jackdaws.

When we reached Chanctonbury itself, I was surprised to discover that inside the ring of beeches and pines was darkness on a sunny summer's day. I shook off Winnie's shadow and disappeared for a moment into the foliage. I found a felled trunk — a precursor to the storm. I sat on it and, not for the first time, left my body and levitated.

I first had this experience walking home through fresh snow. I was five or six years old and lost all track of time, wandering around the corner to where I knew a red wheelbarrow lay buried. Despite the cold of an Upstate New York winter, I felt strangely warm, and my senses zeroed in on the crackling of the snow, as though I could see each flake crunch in my mitten or under my boot. I felt it, too, that spring when I somersaulted down the small verge of grass at the front of our house and lay reveling, digging into the dirt. Time slowed. I stared at the crisp fragility of a blade of grass, rolled between thumb and forefinger. The air around me turned viscous, its molasses-haze making each movement a swim-stroke. Then I floated above to see my shorts-and-T-shirt self below flipping that blade of grass over and over.

The viscous air

This is what happened at Chanctonbury as a child alone among the trees, and as an adult the day I saw my grandmother's apparition. I have had this out-of-body experience throughout my life, whether falling asleep in my bedroom to my father's voice or waking at five in the morning to stare at the streelit glare of an empty intersection outside my window. It's a slowing of the heart rate, a warming in the chest, a numbing of the fingertips. It's the feeling of being swallowed, drowning in the world until I drift out and upwards. It usually happens without warning. But it always happens at Chanctonbury.

Father wore it too The Morris men had stopped dancing and were standing in a rough circle. Several had pulled slips of paper from backpacks; the others knew the words by heart as they began to sing:

Take no scorn to wear the horn
It was the crest when you was born
Your father's father wore it
And your father wore it too

Hal-an-tow, jolly rumbalow
We were up, long before the day-O

To welcome in the summer
To welcome in the May-O
The summer is a-comin' in
And winter's gone away-O

Day was forming, recklessly blue after the early-morning haze. It was no later than eight o'clock by the time the Morris men finished. The sun began to stretch its rays and, as it broke through, the numbness quit my fingertips. Like that, the calendar had turned and it was summer.

I slipped away — no one knew me and no one noticed I was gone, unless Winnie was still watching. I skipped down the hillside, along the tapering tracks favored by mountain bikers, until the land leveled off, and then I headed north towards the tiny church hidden at the foot of Chanctonbury Down.

§

The rabbit had been killed recently and thoroughly. I'm not familiar with rabbit anatomy, and won't take wild guesses, so we'll leave it at this: while the head and the hind were intact, its midsection was split in half and various blood-black bulbs (Its gall bladder? Its spleen?)

Survival of old rites

were distributed as far as six feet from the body. A cruel fate, and only a few days after Easter. One given over to divination with entrails may have noted that the entrails pointed south, towards Chanctonbury, and east, to Steyning — was it a guide, or a warning? Like the nervous wreck dismissed by foolhardy protagonists in a monster movie, I thought, *Whatever killed this rabbit was interrupted — and it's coming back.*

The rabbit's corpse was positioned between yew trees and gravestones in the churchyard, a still life to break up the bright blue skies and drowsy atmosphere. The Ring was visible a mile and a half beyond. Two horses stood with their heads hanging over a fence, their occasional neighs the only sound breaking the drone of light wind and gurgle from a nearby spring.

I had walked a mile north from Chanctonbury and crossed the A283 to reach the gathering of occasional houses that passes for the hamlet of Buncton. There, I climbed a small path over springwater and through a bluebell knoll to the top of a hill before I strolled into the shadow of the single-bell perch of All Saints.

On a ledge within the chancel arch, the plain architecture of this 900-year-old church is broken:

checkered squares in rows, followed by chevrons — 'as if the craftsman has been feeling his way,' or so the church's rubric reads. The designs seemed random, an apprentice trying out untested skills far from any critical eye. The second capital is plain, the lack of parallel uncanny. 'The figure lying down may represent the carver himself.'

Below the chevrons is an empty space just a few inches tall and half a foot long. Once there had been a carving of a figure in this space, a figure lying on its side, legs spread wide apart. At some point, its genitalia had been carefully scraped away by puritanical minds; originally, they would've been preposterous in size and shape, whether it was male or (more likely) female. This was the Buncton sheela na gig.

Sheela na gigs are strange, sexualized, gargoyle-like carvings that can be found in medieval structures around Britain and Ireland. They are humanoid figures, usually female, pushing forward their exaggerated genitalia— a celebration (or admonition) of the sexually curious. It may even be a reference to, or legacy of, a pre-Christian rite. To find an extant sheela na gig in Sussex is rare, and today there is one fewer than there used to be. What had begun with the defacement of the sheela's genitals in centuries past was finished in 2004. At the end of that year someone entered the church at night with a ladder and a chisel and destroyed the carving completely. There were no clues, no leads, nothing to be done. Now the Buncton sheela na gig exists only in photographs and memories.

Like so much of the English landscape, Buncton is a trans-historical mutt. Its name is Saxon (from *Biohchandoune* — 'Birch Down') and the church itself incorporates chunks of Roman tiling from a local villa. But the site, the hill as a location for habitation and exaltation, goes back much further. Before the church was built (1150); before the first historical record of the place (791); before the Roman tiles.

'In the choice of the summit of a hill for this solemn function,' Arthur Stanley Cooke wrote of Buncton in his 1923 book *Off the Beaten Path in Sussex*, 'one seems also to see the survival of old rites, which began in pagan times, and did not entirely change with the advent of Christianity. It was in matters spiritual rather than temporal, that the Church at first sought to win for Christ, and not by too drastic change of sacred customs ... One may regard the hill-top as being as near to Christ as to Wodin. The spirit of the worship was essential.'

Cooke doesn't mention the sheela na gig, but there's little doubt that he saw it, nor that it inspired his relating of Buncton to 'pagan times'.

The church was practically empty. A dozen or so pews, seats for perhaps 60 parishioners, were furnished with a few copies of *Songs of Praise*, various editions of the *New International Bible*, the obligatory picture postcards (4 for £1) and a guest book (one signature per day in high season). Behind a curtain in the back of the church: a few extra flower vases, a broom, a first-aid kit, the fuse box for the electric chandeliers. And nothing else. There was nowhere to hide. Surely even I could find God here.

Der-vish whistle of wind

I sat for a while in one of Buncton's pews, staring at a wall on which a section of medieval decoration had been revealed from beneath the whitewash — a repeated fleur-de-lys pattern. It's as though a hole had been opened in the history of the space. From the bluebells to the eviscerated rabbit, the fleur-de-lys and raggedy brooms, Buncton brimmed with 'the spirit of the worship'. Each detail retained something of all its previous incarnations, as though set aside as a display of England's layered history. And contrary to its destroyer's intentions, the missing sheela was part of this palimpsest. The roughly hewn gap where she had once lain had become, like the peeled-wall design or the devastated trees that peered from Chanctonbury, another spirit added to Buncton's swirling maze.

I sat for nearly an hour. The Chapel was cozy despite cold walls, and her *musique concrète* was settling — the neighing horses, twittering birds, rustling yews. I was phasing in and out of attention, tired from an early start, when the latch at the door fiddled open. In walked a middle-aged man with a long, thin case. We exchanged pleasantries, neither of us expecting to see another in Buncton Chapel on a weekday morning in Ordinary Time. After a few moments, the man settled below the chancel — directly below the empty space of the sheela — and took from his case the unexpected, straight body of a soprano saxophone.

The saxophone of your imagination is the tenor or the alto. It is the slick, curved instrument that provided the lurid, smoky sounds of Dexter Gordon, the amphetamine bebop of Charlie Parker, the abstractions of Ornette Coleman. It is the spiritual tool used in John Coltrane's *A Love Supreme*. The soprano is an instrument of improvisatory abstraction too, but it is one of a contemplative, patient tone: the reedy, philosophical flights of Coltrane's *My Favorite Things*. The tenor is a hawk's plummet and soar; the soprano, a kestrel's red-eyed hover.

The band struck up: the saxophone slurred to heights and stepped back down *pizzicato*, while outside, the horses added their neighs, the wind rolled through the yews. The oaken door creaked as I busied myself between church and churchyard. Buncton became bright with life, reedy vibrato and guttural lowing and spindly chirrup reverberating around the columns.

The musician's name was Peter Pick, and he has played the music of the Downs for decades. In the 1980s, he lived with a damaged-jazz-postpunk band at Iford, a tumbledown manor farm in the Ouse valley south of Lewes. The band, Live Sex, honed a unique sound out of synths, guitars and lyrics about feral disassociation and shattered love. Their music proved critically appealing and commercially unviable. Pick never stopped. Today he releases monthly barrages of improvised MP3s, sometimes including pieces concocted in isolated downland churches.

Pick told me that his Lewes flat is too modest, and

too close to other people, to practice saxophone all day long. So to rehearse, he ventures out to small chapels in the South Downs, off-the-beaten-path and usually empty. Pick plays the sax, but he also plays the church, each one possessing its particular acoustics. He plays their birdsongs, heard on the walk up the path, or their layers of history peeling from the walls, finding a deep tone that resonates with the architecture and working it again and again. The dervish whistle of the wind, mirrored in runs of tones, the keys scuttling like mouse paws on the stone floor.

Each time I tried to leave I was pulled back by a sudden change in tone: a cloud passing overhead, a flurry of notes leveled out into the warm prayer of a long tone; birds cooing and so, too, the sax. The Chapel breathed. When I finally walked away, Pick still resonating behind me, something had changed about the dead rabbit. Parts of its remains had been pulled a few feet to the side. Whatever it was, I thought, it had returned.

x PURGATORIES

A Ghost Walk Through Steyning

WALKING EAST FROM BUNCTON I followed the same path that Hilaire Belloc describes in *The Four Men*: around the foot of Chanctonbury; past Wiston House, ancient seat of the Gorings and their arboreal tendencies; and into Mouse Lane, the deep road I'd taken as a child with my grandmother. Somewhere along this path, Belloc had slept — it is where 'dead friends visited me in dreams'. It was, it *is*, it *long has been*, a ghost path.

Halfway along Mouse Lane lies a stone inscribed with a poem written in 1916, in the trenches of northern France. 'The Steyning Poem', as it is locally known, commemorates this 'lane that goes from Steyning to the Ring'; it was long assumed its author, Philip Johnson, never returned from the war.

Beast of prey

> I never knew till now that those days were so fair
> So we assault in half an hour, and — it's a silly thing —
> I can't forget the narrow lane to Chanctonbury Ring

Johnson's poem is called 'Chance Memory' — an allusion to Chanctonbury's malleable local name: Changebury, Chanckbury, Chancbury. And it gives us Chanctonbury as an escape route. I imagine this terrified young man crouched in a trench, attempting to transfigure the earthen walls of the frontline into those of Mouse Lane: barbed wire becoming root, shrapnel-whistling air becoming lark song. It is not an innocent poem. It is angry. And it is the author, not his surroundings, that changes. 'I am made a beast of prey,' writes Johnson — he is no longer the field mouse but the kestrel, hovering in murderous anticipation. 'This trench is my lair.'

That was not his only transformation. Philip Johnson (sometimes Johnstone) was the pen-name of John Stanley Purvis. He did survive the assault, and many more. Two years later the nostalgic young man was a hardened veteran. His masterpiece, 'High Wood', is a cynical piece of writing in the Modernist spirit. The poet imagines a guide leading visitors on a paid tour of the Somme battlefield on which many of Johnson's comrades died. His prediction came true almost immediately — tourist guidebooks to the battlefields were in print by at least 1919.

> You are requested kindly not to touch
> Or take away the Company's property

As souvenirs; you'll find we have on sale
A large variety, all guaranteed.
As I was saying, all is as it was,
This is an unknown British officer,
The tunic having lately rotted off

At the poem-stone, country lane begins its slow fade and the bustling town of Steyning begins. At first, as Mouse Lane settles from high-walled hollow-way into a regular road, it's nothing more than a few houses with thatched roofs and small gardens. I walked Steyning like a ghost tour — a guided walk of a lost neighbourhood or a battlefield. I was searching for the sights you cannot see.

Beneath clock hands

Steyning's clock tower is a few blocks south along the High Street from Mouse Lane. The essence of a countryside market town, the tower is the place where the soft time of the Downs, governed by hazy light at dawn and dusk, becomes the edged time of the town's clock hands.

Although I never lived there, many of my youthful firsts are stored on its streets: my first bet, placed at a chain bookies; my first cigarette, an illicit Silk Cut achieved at an uncle's expense; my first pints at the White Horse and Chequer Inn, 15th-century coach houses mentioned by

Belloc. My grandfather was the first man I saw dying — bound to his chair, his lungs pockets full of blackness, clinging to dignity in his suit and tie. Entering Steyning from Mouse Lane, passing the poem-stone, joining the High Street, reaching the clock tower — it is, for me, an exercise saddled with strangeness.

I passed a large white house with lace curtains in its front windows. This structure was once the Steyning Register Office where, on 25th June 1891, the shamed Irish statesman Charles Stewart Parnell married his mistress, Kitty O'Shea. Their affair had cost Parnell his position and Ireland its leader — when they rode into Steyning from Brighton to marry, the pair carried with them the shattered dreams of Irish nationalists.

One of those, the poet W.B. Yeats, found solace in Steyning. Parnell had died within months of marrying. Yeats — who engaged with the occult his entire life — must have imagined the statesman's ghost along the High Street when he lived in the town near the end of his life. I curved around the roundabout at the former Registry Office, up Church Street and past the Norfolk Arms to Chantry House. Part-16th-century, part-Georgian, the walls separating its rooms appear wavy from the outside, like a warped photograph, so the building seems to visibly buckle before you. As if it is crouching under the weight of its own history.

For much of the 20th century this was the home of journalist and socialite Edith Shackleton Heald. Yeats spent several months with Heald at Chantry House; he wrote many of his famous final works in a back room of the house, when not off on daily drives through the Downs with Edith. Just a few years ago an old man of Steyning recalled, from his childhood, a white-haired man who wandered the streets muttering, 'Cast a cold eye, on life, on death...'

Before one visit to Steyning, Yeats awoke from a nightmare and wrote to Heald:

> I have a one-act play in my head, a scene of tragic intensity, but doubt if I will begin it till I get to Steyning ... I am so afraid of that dream. My recent work has greater strangeness and I think greater intensity than anything I have done. I never remember the dream so deep.

The play he wrote at Chantry House, *Purgatory*, comes with a single-line setting: 'A ruined house and a bare tree in the background.' In *Purgatory*, an old man already

*Invis-
ibly
reborn*

guilty of patricide kills his only son — the severing of both beginnings and endings — in order to cleanse his lineage of old sins. He is relegated to a living limbo, no history and no future. 'The dead,' wrote Yeats, 'suffer remorse and re-create their old lives just as I have described'. Within months, Yeats himself was dead. The intensity of the dream so deep.

After Yeats' death, Heald took another artistic soul as lover, intellectual partner and cohabitant at Chantry House — the androgynous painter Gluck. Born Hannah Gluckstein into a very wealthy family (heirs to the J. Lyons & Co. fortune) and briefly known as 'Peter', Gluck abhorred gender specificity, dressed in suits and smoked cigars, demanding to be known as 'Gluck, no prefix, suffix or quotes'. Today Gluck's most famous paintings are self-portraits.

The artist's pull on others was powerful. Gluck had a 'wife' — long-term partner Nesta Obermer — but the relationship dissolved as the painter entered Heald's sphere; it was finally severed by the move to Chantry House. Gluck would never fully recover from this mutual yet miserable dissolution. Decades later, Gluck would still be able to write of Nesta, 'Count only this — my heart belongs to thee.'

Gluck's fame today is largely due to an attitude towards gender that was ahead of its time, but it's the artworks that haunt me. Gluck's work veers from technical still lives to uncanny self-portraits and eerie landscapes of the Downs. At the end of Gluck's life, it became surreal, dominated by images of death and decay. In 'Credo (Rage, Rage Against the Dying of the Light)', a painting made only a few years before Gluck's death in 1978, the artist had been walking along the beach in Worthing and discovered the decomposing body of a fish. It is Gluck's masterpiece, swirling with bone whites and earth-grave browns.

'I am living daily with death and decay, and it is beautiful and calming,' Gluck wrote of 'Credo'. 'All order is lost; mechanics have gone overboard — a phantasmagoric irrelevance links shapes and matter. A new world evolves with increasing energy and freedom soon to be invisibly reborn within our airy envelope.'

When I was a child I used to think the massive oak door of St Andrew's church, a few dozen steps from Chantry House, was built for a Cyclops or Grendel, not a human

A new terror

being. I gripped the sanctuary ring compulsively. Just inside, I knew, were steps leading down to the nave. That's where the priest had stood the last time I'd walked into that church, greeting us for my grandmother's funeral service.

I turned from the church door without opening it. Across the churchyard from the entrance I stopped to pull the grass from my grandparents' grave, clearing the soil and weeds that obscured their names. It seemed so tidy: a memorial stone marking their presence, a square foot or so of grass. But for each of them, the end was full of 'phantasmagoric irrelevance'. My grandfather once fell while he was trying, in the depths of illness, to make a tray of afternoon tea and take it to Winnie. In his mind, he was still a young man caring for a younger bride. The last meal I had with Winnie in her Steyning home was fish and chips from the local stand. I poured her a taste of lager and watched her savor the few sips she allowed herself — the last, I'm sure, she ever had. Then I reminded her again which one of her sons was my father. A few days later, as I was leaving, I pressed my cheek against hers and a smile broke from her lips. It didn't matter which one I was.

With Winnie's passing, the last of her generation in my family, Steyning was burdened with a new meaning. It became, for me, a purgatory: a place in between the world in which we now live and the one that only they remembered. It became a marker; a place where 'the dead re-create their old lives' through my memories of them, their confusions and, eventually, their 'phantasmagoric irrelevance'.

I returned to the street and, a few dozen footsteps further, was in Winnie and Bob's cul-de-sac. Theirs was the dead-end house, a postwar suburban family home. As a kid I would play around on the carpets and stand up smelling of dog's hair and tobacco smoke. One August day, aged 11, I sat on that floor — there was tea and fruit squash. There were tiny sandwiches. I can clearly see my grandfather, the way I always remember him,, dressed in shirt, tie and jacket, sitting in his giant easy chair, hands busied with a constant rotation of objects: newspaper, cigarette, tea, repeat.

Ronald Reagan was on TV:

My fellow Americans, I'm pleased to tell you that today I've signed legislation that will outlaw Russia forever. We begin bombing in five minutes.

It was just a politician's gaffe — one of the more
memorable entries in the not-knowing-the-mic-was-
on hall of fame. But my generation had been inducted,
unwittingly, into a nuclear cult of decay, and to us this felt
like the fulfilling of prophecy. In the lingering moment
after I heard his words, a new terror entered my life. So
I made a deal with my imagination. I'd be safe in Britain
while America burned, and I would live in Steyning
forever.

Part of me has kept my end of the bargain.

XI DRAWINGS

Cissbury Ring, As Above So Below

ON THE STEPS OUTSIDE WORTHING RAILWAY STATION, office girls bantered over breakfast cigarettes. It was like a 1980s sitcom; a general nicotine gloom covered the area.

"He stopped texting me and I still texted him and it made me feel so *sschupid*."

"I know everyone's going to say this, but, He. Is. Not. Good. Enough. For. You. Where did he take you, anyway? That new Chinese, yeh? Not. Good. Enough."

The day had just begun, and yet it felt as though the whole town was in a late-afternoon shadow, the final hours of office life when you can't go home but can't raise a give-a-damn either.

The Number 1 bus goes through neighborhoods of Worthing I'd never seen before: neighborhoods of the living. I know one route in the town well, a quiet walk from the station down a winding series of streets. Streets named for poets, counties and cities past their prime. Dotting these streets are large, stately care homes with suburban eponyms etched onto flint-white signs: Restingshrub Manor; Caringcare Lodge; Prettyflowers. They are ubiquitous: once, visiting Winnie Hopper just after she had moved to Worthing, I went to the wrong building and was met with the well-rehearsed response,

"Have you tried next door?"

In her nineties, Winnie had finally succumbed to old age and lost her cherished independence. She moved from her Steyning house into a care home. The first time I saw her there was a shock because, for the only time in her life, she had neither of those pillars of her character: domesticity and independence. For more than a decade, Winnie had fought against the odds to stay at home, cook her own meals, paint her watercolors, talk to the birds in the garden. In Worthing, she was cared for by others for the first time since the mid-1930s. She would rather have died. So she did.

Within a few minutes the Number 1 was out of the center of Worthing, rolling through neighborhoods of trim lawns and semi-detached — then, detached — houses. As a child I had walked Worthing's beaches with my family. I knew it as a beachfront and a deathbed and was embarrassingly surprised to see an abundance of normal life: Brighton commuters closing their garden gates; kids setting off on their bikes; daytime drinkers getting down to business. I left the bus at Findon Valley, a dry-river dene with a suburb deposited in it. It sticks out like a little splash of grey accidentally painted outside the lines of Worthing's footprint. There is a bottleneck in the town's north-bound road, the A24, where Worthing should end, and Findon Valley is the squeezed eruption beyond. Following the gardens and houses east, it becomes a car park and, just beyond, a gentle slope that signals the rise of Cissbury Ring.

On a map it looks like a partner to Chanctonbury, just across the valley; twin sentinels marking the halfway point between the coast at Beachy Head and Winchester. From the escarpment on its northern side, Cissbury is pure downland; a bulbous mass; not as dramatic, perhaps, as its sister but more sprawling. A satellite image bears this out. Chanctonbury is a circle, as obvious as it could be. Cissbury, on the other hand, spreads out like an amoeba, a warren of paths and pockmarks leading to a sudden sheer wall at the northeastern corner. It is well-worn. It is lived-in. And that's because of the flint.

Because we trip over it on every downland walk, it's easy to overlook the earthshaking qualities of flint. In the technological arms race that dominated this island 10,000 years ago, flint was the fuel that drove human change.

Of the properties of flint, there is one that borders on the magical. Each sample of this common sedimentary rock, wrote the 19th-century Sussex geologist Gideon Mantell, possesses 'what in mineralogical language is called a *cleavage*, or peculiar fracture, which is distinct in each. Thus, if I take a flint and break it at random, you perceive that it presents a glassy or *conchoidal* fracture, a sharp cutting edge; and subdivide it as I may, it still retains the same character ... so true is the remark, that we cannot break a stone but in one of nature's joinings.'

Flint is sharp and it is strong and it cannot help but be so. Once it's been worked — *knapped* in the parlance of today, flaking away at a lump of flint until it's a useful shape and size — into something you can hold, or tie to an axe handle, you've got a tool that will last far beyond your own lifetime.

The Downs are full of bands of flint locked into the chalk: rivers and lakes of them. Even today, you can stumble over chunks of the stuff. But to obtain flint in significant amounts you have to dig. And 4,000 years ago, that's what they were doing at Cissbury. The site was bustling with men and women, lowering themselves into shafts dug into the side of the hill to scrape away at the chalk, carving out nodules of flint to be carried back and worked on the surface. There were an incredible number of working pits on Cissbury — at least 60, probably many more.

One day, a 20-year-old woman was lowered into one of these mineshafts. Let's identify it — let's call it Shaft 27. At the bottom, more than 15 feet below the earth's surface, she scanned the shaft for a starting point, lighting the walls with a small taper she carried with her. She decided on a spot — a small gallery from which other miners had successfully culled lumps of flint — and began scraping at the walls with her pick-axe, an engineered red deer's antler. She had other objects: a container, something with which to raise her finds back to the surface. There were marks on the walls from other antler-tools — not just cuts to remove flint, but lines scrawled on the gallery walls and the sides of the pit. They were small comforts, flickering in the taper-light.

The taper was still in her hand when she died — when the first block of chalk smashed her face. Other blocks crushed her chest and broke her back. We can hope it was a sudden death — that the first, mortal blow came swiftly, before she knew it was happening. Whatever the case, her body, locked into a permanent grotesque twist, lay untouched for the following 4,000 years. Perhaps Shaft 27 was declared dangerous by her colleagues, or haunted. Maybe it was understood to be a grave. But for whatever reason, it was closed up and forgotten. A few hundred years later, the miner's descendants camped above it, oblivious. They tossed the chewed ox and pig joints from their campfire into the pit, where those bones rested, on top of the rubble that hid her remains.

For all those centuries, she remained, ignored, until a kind and gentle man in a waistcoat and rolled-up sleeves arrived to exhume the body and give her peace.

Spirits of forgotten folk In the 1920s a young man named John Henry Pull walked the Downs around Cissbury and saw it the way it had once been seen. It's an ancient landscape: a ley line of flint mines stretches just above Worthing — Harrow Hill, Church Hill, Blackpatch, Cissbury. But in Pull's day these sites were still virtually unrecognized.

Pull was only 23 years old when he made his first archaeological discovery, but he'd already lived many lives and they hadn't always been kind. Born in June 1899 in Arundel, just down the river of forgetfulness from Amberley, by the age of 16 Pull was finished with formal education and a year later, thanks to a lie about his age, on his way to fight in Europe with the Rifle Corps. He was good at it — a natural leader of men, but, unfortunately for the King's Corps, already a profoundly moral one. Offered promotion to officer rank, the teenager refused on the grounds that he would not order men into a certain-death situation, no matter how tactically important it was. The military couldn't handle that, and Pull stayed in the lower ranks. He was injured in a German gas attack, captured, escaped and found his way to a Belgian convent where he holed up for the rest of the war. Isolated, they didn't know the war had ended. Pull struck out for home, sneaking past Dutch border guards before discovering he needn't have bothered.

Once back home in Worthing, Pull began reading obsessively about archaeology, teaching himself the burgeoning field's theories and practices. He also discovered that he had to be outside — had to be walking, for his lungs, permanently impaired by the German gas. He got a job as a postman, and spent weekends up on the Downs; evenings were for reading about his new love, archaeology. In 1922, he strode out onto the hills, looking for a new walk to add to his repertoire. That day, he walked Blackpatch, near Findon and west of Cissbury, where he was struck by a vision.

> As one climbs the hill a vista of open, rolling downland unfolds on all sides. Green, undulating slopes and mist-clouded coombes stretch to right and left, mile after mile, into the hazy distance. Nowadays truly an uninhabited land filled with the turf-carpeted remains of bygone civilizations, and peopled with the spirits of long-forgotten folk. Paleolithic hunter, Neolithic herdsman, Iberian miner, Beaker chieftain, Bronze Age Alpine, Iron Age Celt, Roman, Saxon and Norman, all have lived and died here. … The whole clearing was thickly studded with saucer-shaped depressions … I immediately realized that I had stumbled across a hitherto unexamined, and, so far as I knew, unrecorded site.

Pull took matters into his own hands; he gained permission from the Duke of Norfolk, who owned the land, and began to dig. Alone. It wasn't long before he realized that the task before him was bigger and more important than one man could handle in his spare time. Pull called on the Worthing Archaeological Society to lend its manpower and know-how. Together, they uncovered a vast complex of flint mines, flaking floors, dwelling sites and barrows.

It was the turning point in Pull's young career. Years into the Blackpatch digs, when it came time to publish the results, the Society — comprised of professionals as well as aspiring amateurs — rejected Pull's report on the site. They pushed him out of the publishing process altogether, rewriting his notes and redrawing his images of the site. The site that he had seen in a vision, discovered in the ground and excavated with his own hands.

This betrayal would have a long impact on Pull. He continued as a weekend-and-evening archaeologist, outside of the academic mainstream. Whilst Blackpatch became a key archaeological site for southern England, Pull moved on — he continued excavations with his own teams of volunteers, barely breaking for the Second World War when he worked for the Local Defence Volunteers and in a still-unknown capacity for a Sussex-based intelligence unit.

By the early 1950s, Pull had a new vision: he would dig the flint mines at Cissbury. His dream was yet unfulfilled, to come face-to-face with one of the miners from all those thousands of years ago. Maybe here. Maybe at Cissbury. So in the spring of 1953, Pull dug open a mine pit. He had identified 64 of them as potential targets, but this was a prime candidate — Shaft 27. Eleven feet into the shaft, he found strange objects: an ox skeleton and pig bones; flint knives; axes. He kept going. A few feet further down, in the entrance to one of the mine galleries, there it was: a human skeleton, traces of charcoal present in its right hand from a torch or a small candle.

'The find of the century!' Pull wrote in his notes. He wrote carefully but excitedly, describing his archaeological discoveries like an old friend. Pull cared about this person he'd found. The skeleton is never merely 'it', never merely a skeleton, always 'his bones' and 'his remains'. When it was later determined on examination that this was a female skeleton, Pull went through his personal notebook and in every instance carefully crossed out 'he' and 'his' and wrote 'she' and 'her'.

Shaft 27 *was* a once-in-a-century find, but not because of the skeleton. Digging further, Pull made another discovery: prehistoric graffiti. Some were complex symbols, but without obvious meaning. Pull called them 'miners' signs'; he imagined them as informational, perhaps declaring a gallery to be plentiful, exhausted or dangerous. Some were representational drawings, in the way we understand that concept. A deer. A bull. A fish.

Unmistakable.

Pull made rubbings and sketches of the chalk carvings. That's all we've got, since Pull wasn't the kind of guy who would carve an image out from its tomb. And it's more than enough.

There is the head of a red deer depicted in profile. Its antlers and proud jaw are clear in Pull's rubbings and drawings and it is carefully rounded at the nose; an eye, patiently inscribed. There is a short-horned bull, pulling its head and neck upwards in a gesture of strength. These are arguably the more important discoveries to archaeology, but the one that most captured Pull's attention is also the one that beckons me today. It's one of the miners' signs he describes, but this one Pull gives a name: 'the star-spread indefinite flint mark'.

This is a shape-shifting mark; a Rorschach inkblot. Each time I look at it, it appears to have changed. There is a thick line down the center with protrusions either side — similar to a stick figure — and a pair of other marks floating above. It could be a figure with a head, or a pickaxe made from a deer's antler, like the tool with which it was probably made. It could be a pair of arms raised to the surface world or the heavens above it. It could just as easily be the random results of a pick dragged along the gallery wall.

I love the star spread indefinite because Pull loved it, an unrecognizable scratch to which he gave that grand title. And I love it, too, for the reason I believe he did: Even with a torch or taper, it must have been made in near darkness, the artist feeling her way along the gallery wall. She scratched at the chalk, eking out a sign with no reason to believe anyone would ever see it. Yet she left it anyway to announce her presence — a mark to say 'I lived'.

At least half-way

The last time I saw my grandmother alive, I walked into her room in the Worthing care home and she greeted me with outstretched arms. "I've just seen you on the telly," she said, glowing. She hadn't. To her, any man with glasses was either myself or my father.

Winnie had been drawing when I arrived that day. Always a fine artist, she had excelled at watercolors, but now that was beyond her. Sketching figures from the newspaper seemed like more than just a way to pass the time. It was an act of independence, a sliver of self-control remaining for a woman whose time had gone, but whose stubbornness had kept her alive. Sitting on her desk in the old folks' home was a drawing of a man, sketched from the newspaper. It was perfect, identical to the photograph in form, in shading, in every way but one. Her drawing was exactly half-formed, the image's right-hand side, as though it had been cut down the middle and the left-hand side discarded. I imagined how difficult a proposition that would be for someone who had *meant* to do it. For Winnie it hadn't been purposeful, but a signal — her mind, her hand, stopping each line exactly halfway thanks to some invisible, internal logic. *I'm here, at least halfway.*

"I met a man yesterday," Winnie said. It stopped me in my tracks. I knew it wasn't true. "I was out hitchhiking. In Scotland. And I met a man. He was so handsome. It was late, getting dark, and I was worried I wouldn't get back to the village, but he picked me up by the side of the road — a very quiet road, very pretty. And we talked the whole way.

She went on at length about the night, the man, how kind he was, how handsome. Nothing untoward, mind you, only kindness; nothing more or less than a lift for a woman in distress on a dark Scottish road. Was it a memory or a confusion, a TV police procedural seen the night before comingling with her reality? Was it an invention, to fill a gap with which her heart couldn't cope?

There was no ignoring the joy. It would be the last moment of Winnie's joy that I experienced; I'll never know if there were more moments of such purity for her, and who am I to deny it? If it was joy from the dreamtime, rather than the 'real', is that any less valid? The drawing, the story — these misfirings of the mind stay with me as oddly triumphant final memories of my grandmother. In her final, darkening days, she still sought to leave a mark.

The bull the deer John Pull's legacy should be the drawings he discovered. But thanks to his difficult relationship with academic archaeology, the Shaft 27 findings were never officially published until two contemporary archaeologists, Miles Russell and Anne Teather, recognizing his importance, sought to redress the loss of Pull's work. Teather goes so far as to conclude that, not only were Pull's carvings authentic — there was widespread skepticism among the field in the '50s — they're also practically unique. Her conclusion is that the carvings are, indeed, at least 4,000 years old, and that the representational pieces — the bull, the deer — are almost unparalleled from that period.

But by the time Russell and Teather began to publish

their work on Pull he was 40 years dead, his demise as strange as his life. In 1960, having retired from the post office but needing to fund his archaeological work, the 61-year-old Pull took a job as security guard at a bank in Durrington, a couple of miles from Cissbury Ring. On 10th November, Pull and a clerk were alone in the branch. At just past 10 a.m. Pull had gone into the office to boil a kettle when a 20-year-old west London Teddy Boy-cum-gangster named Victor Terry walked in with a shotgun under his drape jacket. Pull came out of the office just as Terry had moved to the safe with the clerk, now, unbeknownst to Pull, a hostage.

Something happened. Pull might have touched Terry; just as likely, it was nothing — a gasp, an involuntary quake of the hand. It doesn't much matter. Victor Terry was jittery from nerves and pills — drinamyl, the uppers known as purple hearts that became the calling card of Mod subculture. Terry jumped. He was probably feeling crazed anyway because of what had happened in the car. On the radio, minutes before he entered the bank, he'd heard the news that gang associates and childhood friends Flossie Forsyth and Norman Harris were, at that very moment, dangling at the end of the hangman's noose, executed for murder. Whatever the cause, Terry's reaction was to swivel the shotgun out and blast Pull through the eye. He was dead before he hit the ground.

Terry and his girlfriend fled the scene but were captured a few days later in Glasgow, recognized after a manhunt that made the front pages of the nationals. In what must be one of the most bizarre legal defense arguments in British history, Terry claimed that Pull's murder couldn't be pinned on him because it wasn't him. The spirit of long-dead American bootlegger Legs Diamond had possessed Terry; it was Diamond's fault. In May 1961, Terry was hanged for the murder of John H Pull.

Besides the Legs Diamond defense, Terry blamed his own drug addiction — citing 'diminished responsibility' — in a case that revealed to Britain the extent of its suburban underworld. Even after the execution, the murder continued to make headlines. In the 1960s, the movement to abolish the death penalty used Terry's case to attack its efficacy. After all, what deterrent was the death penalty if this man had killed within an hour of hearing that his close friend had dangled for the same crime?

There is a photograph of John H Pull the day he found the miner's skeleton. He is standing in the pit, looking up at the camera, his hair slicked back from his forehead and his sleeves rolled up, pipe in hand. His is the joy of completing a mission, of having come face-to-face with those people he had imagined three decades beforehand. He had found the humanity at the root of all those pits and chalk scrapings, the flint axes and expired charcoal tapers. He had found the human beings, and found the marks they left — star-spread half drawings left on an indefinite landscape.

I circled up the steeper part of the mount to where one can look out towards Chanctonbury. I could clearly see the path of the Great Storm of 1987 from that vantage point — where it had meandered through Chanctonbury's trees, uprooting in an improvised arc. I descended to the plain that connects Cissbury and Chanctonbury. A hundred meters or so along the road between them, I entered a dumpsite crowned by the shell of an annihilated car. Age and weather had given it a new kind of color: a hard rust with yellowish white accents, both inside and out. Water pooled in the curved-in roof. The front hood was missing,

Brimming with bonfire ash

and weeds grew through the chassis; it was buried a few inches into the ground. The tops of the axles were peeking out over the dirt. It was being reclaimed, swallowed by the earth.

It had, in a previous incarnation, been a hatchback, but the entire back had been ripped off to reveal a spare-tyre well filled with crushed cans — energy drinks and lager. They were on the seats, too, and surrounding the car. A flatbed trailer beside it was in a similar state of reclamation by grass and weeds and hard-drinking youths. Both were brimming with bonfire ash.

XII SIGNS

Reading the Haunted Hills and Shoreline

MY SON THOMAS WAS THREE MONTHS OLD when I strapped him to my chest and walked to the Long Man of Wilmington. We were staying at a house in Milton Street, little more than a handful of structures beside a country lane northwest of Eastbourne. From there, a path cut across open fields to the hamlet of Wilmington. I cupped my hands around Thomas's little head, overcompensating for the minor breeze; in fact, it was hot having him slung tight against me. In those early, growing days, an infant emanates such energy.

The path was a green channel through a field of bristles. Straight along its sightline to the west was the profile of Firle Beacon. The previous night we had watched the sun set behind Firle, its peak afloat in a tangerine glow that filled the valley around us. From the east, Firle appears so velvety and welcoming; I could jump from its crown and bounce like a trampolinist down its slope.

One December, a few years before, on the morning of the winter solstice, some friends from Lewes took me to Firle to trek up that slope before dawn. I watched the others flowing up the hillside in the darkness and mud,

To the four winds

a few dressed in white robes or wearing crowns of holly and thorn. At the top of Firle we joined in a circle. There was music and poetry. The local vicar, his Christian faith unthreatened by such weird stirrings, led an invocation to the four winds and the four elements. We wrote our year's failings or misgivings on pieces of paper and threw them onto a bonfire. There were flasks of hot, mulled wine making the rounds, and a hand drum passed as well. A man in white clothes and a purple cape, a crown on his head, raised his arms, silhouetted against a fiery rising sun.

Most in attendance were people you would pass on the street without noticing. One woman was on the way to her rounds as a postal worker in Lewes; another had her NHS scrubs peeking out from a heavy winter coat. No one mentioned anything particularly religious, no gods or goddesses. The passing of time was marked, the sun welcomed back, and we all got on with our day.

I have kept that sunrise with me. It was cold at the top of Firle Beacon, and that cold bore the glowing, blue-black darkness of the English countryside. On Firle before dawn, that darkness was cracked only by the fading moon reflected on clouds. When the sun appeared, it was as if from nowhere — there was no flicker, no 'first rays', just the sudden panning flame of sun. Soon it was visible as an object, staring at us, coaxing us; I felt like a child, wanting to impress it. On Firle, there was nothing between us and the sky nor us and the land below, a sheet of motley greens squinting into view with the light.

Thomas and I turned from the house at the end of the path, looking out towards Firle, and walked east to Wilmington. When we reached the hamlet and entered the grounds of its church, we were confronted with the commanding presence of a very old and stubborn yew tree. The Wilmington yew is a conjoined tree, two inosculated trunks sharing one base. Stare at its bark, gnarled into smiles and snarls, and you'll find signs reflected back at you — the hollows in its skin mouth words. The yew is some 1,600 years old, taking root not long after the Romans gave up on Britain. Mick had told me that yew trees stand in churchyards to remind us of another way of life. By the time the Long Man was cut into Windover Hill overlooking the church, people had already been making up tales about the Wilmington yew for hundreds of years.

Its skin mouths words

The tree is stubborn, but in need of help. Planks dug

into the ground prop up its 30-foot base; its branches are reined in by thick rope to keep its growth in balance. I approached the tree with the apprehension of a hospital visit and was surprised to place my hand on it and find the knots sturdy and comforting. With my palm pressed against it, insects quickly began exploring my skin. It was an ecosystem, and it thrived.

I placed Thomas's hand there, implausibly new against the bark, and each warmed the other. It would soon be autumn.

Lines in the hillside

I left the churchyard and walked along a path to the foot of the Long Man. Windover Hill extends up out of Wilmington at a soft and grassy 40-degree angle, making it manageable for working on the slope and yet dramatic in its vantage. The Long Man itself stretched out in a gentle sweep before Thomas and I. It is a human figure with no features, no digits, just a simple line drawing, with arms outstretched and a vertical staff at each hand. Originally comprised of simple lines cut into the hillside to expose the white of the chalk, it is more than 20 storeys tall and just as wide. Its has been construed as many things: a pilgrim with two walking sticks, a warrior with spears, or a farmer with tools for tilling; a faceless humanoid pushing open a doorway, or even a ley-line man sighting his straight lines. A catalog's worth of myths and dates have been proposed for the Long Man's origins. Today we think it to be from the late 16th century, but we will likely never know. Today's Long Man is made of white stones placed on the outline of the original — so was the Early Modern figure itself a recreation of something far older?

I had intended to climb to the top — I'd done so before and wanted to take Thomas there on his first foray into the Downs. But at the bottom of this figure it seemed unnecessary — what I wanted was for us to be together on the grass and the chalk, and here we were. I took Thomas from his sling and cradled him, his eyes, unfocused, opening towards the figure.

I returned to the Long Man months later, in the spring, and walked to the top with Adam. Adam was the man I had encountered on the path to the Crossroads outside Amberley. He is a druid, a member of a group of modern pagans who conduct rituals at the Long Man — open rituals that anyone can attend, regardless of belief. Adam

Let me sit beside you

agreed to take me to the Long Man and show me those hillsides the way he sees them after nearly 20 years of solstices, equinoxes and other Celtic holidays.

We met outside Eastbourne. I recognized Adam by his goatee, whitening to chalk. He was wearing a t-shirt that portrayed the intertwined roots of a tree as a DNA double-helix. From the northern edge of Wilmington we walked along the rise and curve of The Street until we reached Wilmington Priory, the last buildings before the settlement peters out into the fields below the Long Man. A group of schoolchildren were just setting off to walk to the figure, so we lagged behind, giving them time to tour and move on. Meanwhile, Adam told me about the day he met the Goddess.

After Adam and I had met on the Old Road, the Goddess had visited him on the Downs between Amberley and Chanctonbury. Adam was walking the Way to celebrate his fiftieth birthday, and was doing so at a manic pace that he pulled a muscle. He was in pain after climbing the chalk pit that marks the ascent out of the Arun Valley past Amberley and up to the easterly ridge. He sat down for a rest and fell asleep.

"I had this sensation of something brushing my cheek

and then a vision of a lady. She said to me, 'Let me sit beside you for a while.' That's all she said. I opened my eyes, and the vision was gone. I had this sense: that was the Goddess, and in that one phrase she told me that I didn't have to prove anything — not to myself, not to the land, not to anybody."

It was, he assured me, the first time he'd been struck by such a direct spiritual intervention. Adam's beliefs fit in with many in the Neo-Druidic tradition — an animist vision of the landscape and staunch environmentalism bolstered by belief, at least metaphorically, in the myths and legends found in the ancient Welsh book *The Mabinogion*. But most of the time, his druidism boils down to something far more simple: an assurance that the landscape is a gift in which we can find strength, and which we must treasure.

The students out of sight, we walked to the foot of the Long Man. There's a kind of ledge below him, favored by the sheep with which he shares Windover Hill, and Adam and I stood there - where we could look up and see the full extent of the figure and, in the opposite direction, down across fields of pasture and crop. Adam's conversion experience — if you can call it that — occurred around this spot. Adam and his wife, Rebekah, attended one of the rituals held by the druid group Anderida Gorsedd. (Anderida Forest is the Roman name for the Weald; Gorsedd, a coming-together of druids and bards.) On the ledge below the Long Man they joined in a circle: the people called on the "hawk of dawn" and the "sacred hills that bear the winds"; invoked the water that surrounds our island as well as its earthen floor. They recited poems and played instruments. Adam was invigorated by this celebration of, and in, the landscape, and inspired by celebrating at this spot — at the Long Man.

That was 17 years ago. Adam and Rebekah, druid and witch, made their way through the world, punctuated with seasonal forays to the Long Man, and always bound together by their relationship to the land. They now have a seven-year-old son, Freddie, a beautiful boy who carries with him a burden.

Adam and I climbed to the top of the Long Man. From the bottom, we might walk across fields or through the churchyard and see the figure loom ahead, getting bigger and bigger as we approach; he hovers into view and is marked for miles. From the top of Windover Hill we came to the edge of the hilltop from behind the exposed-chalk pathway and there he was — the figure pops, crisp and white, from the angle of the hill.

We walked away from the Long Man and towards the northwest, in the direction of Firle Beacon. Adam told me about Freddie. He is a child troubled by anxieties in the form of a particular band of the autistic spectrum known as Pathological Demand Avoidance: he has a ruinous reaction when faced with the demands of everyday life. Freddie is at his happiest when outdoors, free, scrambling along a rocky hill or jumping through the forest or running along the Downs with his father and mother. Walking the paths, visiting the Long Man, the spirituality of the landscape — these aren't just pastimes, but tools Adam and his family use to find solace, if not necessarily answers.

"It's not about solutions. It's a way I can learn to cope with the problems of the world — to deal with the things I can't change, and change the things I can. I've tried yoga, Tai Chi, meditation — but I have trouble getting into that calm state. But walking, especially like the Downs, a path I know well, I get into a trance. It gives me a way to deal with those problems."

I have a friend who, when he found out he was going to be a father, taught himself everything he could about the night sky — the stars, constellations, comets. Then he could always share the sky with his child. Rich or poor, young or old, anywhere in the world the sky would be there and it would belong to them.

I'm looking at a photograph I took of the Long Man the day three-month-old Thomas and I visited Windover Hill, and I can see a new interpretation of the sign drawn on the hillside. It is not farming tools or ley-sighting staves or walking sticks that he is holding in his hands. They are walls crushing in from either side — the ever-present demands and anxieties of our lives. And the figure is Thomas; it is Freddie, Rebekah or Adam. It is me. It stands on the Downs and looks towards Firle Beacon's tangerine flames at sunset and sunrise. There, on the chalk that we walk together and will always share, rich, poor, young, old, the figure pushes back. It holds the walls at bay.

§

The sign behind the counter at Smugglers said: YOU DON'T HAVE TO BE CRAZY TO WORK HERE. WE'LL TRAIN YOU.

Another graced a jar of pickled eggs: SUN RAYS — HAPPY DAYS. I had taken the bus from Brighton, disembarking at Rottingdean for the second day in a row, retracing my steps in reverse down a side street of closed sundries shops and fast food joints towards the beach. The Scientist had told me that Smugglers was one of those fish-and-chips spots worth visiting: greasy, table-less, inexpensive, belt-bustingly good. I would eat their wares on the beach, pulling chunks of buttery fried fish and vinegar-drowned chips into my mouth with hungover fingers, thinking of Barbet Schroeder's *Barfly* — "He's like a goddamn seagull".Or a crow.

Ahead of me in the queue a young woman with raven hair in bunched-up bangs also awaited her order. Beside her was a tiny baby in a pram. She chatted to the woman at the counter and skeletal details emerged. She had an angry dog, making combined baby-and-dog-sitting a difficult sell to her mother. Then there was her boyfriend, another angry creature she had to manage delicately. She was at the end of her rope, yet exuded calm: *I've got this*.

Her chips came, and she reached forward for them. For the first time I noticed that her long, slender middle finger was tattooed: a goat's head with spindly horns and a forked tongue, wings peeking out from behind the skull-like form familiar from Tarot decks and heavy-metal album covers. The rendering was wrong, ratios off due to the slim canvas the artist had been afforded, but nonetheless, it was unmistakable.

While eating my fish, I texted the Scientist to tell him what I'd seen. He responded quickly.

"The signs are always there."

The Scientist is, really, a scientist. He understands the body and the mind and, probably better than most people, the interactions and elisions between the two — it's what he does. What's more, he understands how much we don't know about those interactions. He knows that signs, symbols, portents, can be a trick of the mind, but also a liberation; that the things we see, in the places we choose to look, be that the stars above or the entrails below, might be of grave personal or celestial importance, or misleading, meaningless blather.

The Scientist frequents the edges of Sussex: the chalk cliffs and flinty beaches where the South Downs spill into the English Channel. One day in 2011, walking along the beach at Beachy Head during a tumultuous period in his personal life, the Scientist found a flint shaped and colored like Anubis, the wolf-headed Egyptian god responsible for guiding people to the afterlife; the watchman between two worlds. To a man experiencing hardship, standing in this liminal space — the beach at Beachy Head read as a gateway to purgatory and the terminus of the English landscape — such a vision was loaded with meaning.

I met the Scientist at his home near the coast at Rottingdean, a house brimming with the chaos that thrives at the intersection of suburbia and eccentricity. Clothes, unopened post, toys, food — everything — covered the house in a thin film. But there was a hierarchy at play: family photos, books, reference materials were all kept tidy in their appropriate place.

Around in a spiral

The Scientist is a medical-research professional — he studies the brain and the physical maladies caused or exacerbated by emotional and mental trauma. And, like Adam, he's a middle-aged father. His jet-black hair and serious demeanor must, at one point, have predisposed him to the Gothic side of popular culture. Now that seriousness manifests itself as a keen attentiveness to the world around him — be it the gentle scrutiny of a patient's symptoms, or the reading of a landscape.

We walked to Saltdean, the beach east of Rottingdean where the cliffs are bright white and sheer, and arrived at a small row of doors in front of the cliff face — beach huts for hire. They must be busy on days when there isn't a strong, sunless wind; when beach-walkers aren't wrapped in coats, hats and gloves. There were half a dozen doors on each side of a central white one, each a slightly different shade of faded art-deco glory.

"My whole life I've been of two mindsets," the Scientist said. "One rationalist and one irrational — as a boy, I was fascinated by the supernatural, but as a student I rejected all of that. Now I'm going around in a spiral, becoming less literal — interested in the weird but without being credulous."

After his vision of Anubis at Beachy Head, the Scientist began a new venture — a blog to catalog his seaside discoveries. 'Beachy Head Anubis: Guardian of the Shoreline' was the first post on what became *The Haunted Shoreline*. The goal was to use the landscape alchemically — to decipher the symbols it threw in his path as a means of forging a personal connection to place and, through that, an understanding of the self.

"Before I began this project," the Scientist wrote, "I

had been through a period of immense personal upheaval, and in the aftermath I entered a phase where nothing seemed to hold meaning or value: music, art, science, books... all were dead to me."

What pulled him half out of this state was Ted Hughes' poetry book, *Crow*. For the Scientist, the poems' alchemical blackness hinted at transformations to come; *Crow*'s 'grotesque yet comically futile acts of defiance against higher powers' became a life-giving talisman that gave him purchase on a metaphorical cliff-face — the threshold between land and sea, consciousness and unconsciousness, life and death, form and formlessness.

> He knew he grasped
> Something fleeting
> Of the sea's ogreish outcry and convulsion.

"It's something in that threshold of consciousness," the Scientist told me of the *Shoreline*. "I could sense that there's more — something unseen; something in the unconscious. It's not contrived, it's a way of revealing that which is there. A confluence between my esoteric and scientific interests."

Dreams are private myths

On the beach between Saltdean and Rottingdean
we found a slice of tree trunk that had emerged from the
ocean. On top of the trunk sat a stone, an off-kilter oval
shape with two holes and two indentations on its flat side,
like a face. The holes were perfectly positioned to seem
like sad, drooping eyes; the indentations, like a half-oval
of nose and a squiggled, open mouth. It called to mind
the face in Munch's *The Scream*, but also something more
uncanny.

When the famous escape from Alcatraz took place,
the inmates left behind papier-mâché heads tucked up in
their beds — to delay the guards' discovery of their escape.
I saw these haunting, misshapen masks, their features
stretched and squished, on a childhood visit to Alcatraz
island. Those masks have lurked in the dark corners of my
dreams ever since.

The oval stone reminded me of the masks. They were
like the husks of human beings, discarded when their
owners fled the world.

To decipher his finds, the Scientist uses a litany of sources
and theories — the Western mystery tradition, as well
as its spiritual, philosophical and poetic canon, but also

Egyptian and Eastern mythologies, psychedelia, Dada, surrealism and Jungian analysis. In Jung's methods, the dreams and visions that we encounter are there to be engaged with and, perhaps, understood. The Scientist's symbols are encountered randomly on the shoreline, but he examines them as we might do a dream — or, perhaps, a myth. As Joseph Campbell wrote, 'myths are public dreams; dreams are private myths'.

If I apply the methods of the *Haunted Shoreline* to my find, the Alcatraz Mask Stone, I might discover something about myself. First there is the long history of American mask-wearers: our ubiquitous smile, our demented religiosity. Beyond that there is something more personal: the self that I left behind when I departed America for the UK — a warped mask, the husk of a human, hidden in my lifelong home. Was this discovery, this symbol from the sea, telling me to sever ties to that past? Or to reclaim it?

"Who are you?" asked the stone. I had no answer.

We walked the shoreline back to Rottingdean beach, and the Scientist told me why he had brought the *Haunted Shoreline* to a close. There are limits to what can be achieved through alchemical exploration, he said. And there are limits to what we can stand before we begin to see things too quickly and make connections of the worst kind.

"There are limits to science in the world of human experience," he said, slowly strolling along the beach, pointing to graffiti on a seawall. "Jung defined synchronicity as an 'acausal connecting principle' — and at times of crisis, that synchronicity comes thick and fast."

The Scientist had gone too far with the *Shoreline*. He was becoming troubled by the signs — like Burroughs had said of the city, the 'second-attention awareness' became too much. That acausal connecting principle was everywhere — the shape of every wave and of every piece of driftwood was speaking to the Scientist with associations and self-examination, and it had become cacophonous. He had found his way out of the troubles he'd been living, and it was time for the visions to end.

Masks like flowers That night I dreamt of masks. The stone from the beach was tucked in my jacket pocket, the jacket slumped over a chair in my Brighton hotel room. The masks in my dreams bloomed like flowers, glowing abstracts hanging on the wall of an unassuming room. They were half-formed. And among the masks, one I recognized. It was as though memories, tucked for a generation into the stones of the shoreline below the Downs, had crept into my unconscious. I was beginning to see signs everywhere.

I slept soundly, yet woke exhausted, for I had dreamt of Doris.

XIII SEARCHING FOR DORIS

Part Three

I HADN'T FOUND DORIS, just more questions.

What I had stumbled across was a place of death: Rochford, a small town north of Southend-on-Sea. That meant I could order a copy of Doris Hopper's death certificate. She died, not on an East Sussex shoreline, but in a surgical theatre, suffering from shock during an operation on her knee at General Hospital, Southend, early in 1933. The hospital had only been open a few weeks at that point, and it seemed that the archives for that year had disappeared. No more information was forthcoming. No one in our family had ever heard of my grandfather living in Essex, though he was listed right there on the certificate: Robert Christopher Hatton Hopper of Westcliff-on-Sea. It still didn't add up — and what about Beachy Head?

I had another date: John Hatton Hopper, Doris's only child, had died in February 1931, a few months past his second birthday. It's almost certain that the condition with which he was born was Down Syndrome. In the photos he is a happy child in a happy family — he had a devoted mother and father, a suburban life on the lower rungs of the middle class; he wanted for little. I've composed a picture of his character: he was strong, difficult at times, but more often contagious with joy.

Doris and John compelled me. I wanted to honor that strength and difficulty and joy with a living memory. So I kept looking and I kept walking. And I began to dig elsewhere, in the archive. One day, something hit:

'Beachy Head Fall'.

It was the *Derby Daily Gazette* of 23rd July 1932, reporting on an event the previous evening.

> Mrs Doris Hopper, of Kingscote-road, Addiscombe, Croydon, who was rescued last evening after falling 400 feet down the cliff at Beachy Head, was reported to-day not to be in danger. She will be X-rayed in view of the possibility of injuries not apparent from an ordinary examination.

Kingscote Road, Addiscombe, Croydon. My father was born on Kingscote Road. It was her. At Beachy Head. A fall? Or, perhaps, a leap? When my relatives had spoken of Doris, they had been right. Something had happened.

xiv PILGRIMAGES

Making the Journey to Beachy Head

ONCE THERE WAS A WOMAN who stood at the edge of a cliff.

§

I had been skirting around the issue of Beachy Head. I'd been to the Long Man, five miles to the north, and along the nearby shoreline. I hadn't returned to Beachy Head since discovering the truth about Doris Hopper's incident at the cliffs. But the calendar is a gross instigator. One morning, as I sifted through the details I'd learned about Doris, facts upon which I'd yet to act, I was struck by the date. She'd stood on the edge on 22nd July. That morning was the 21st.

Assembled tokens

I fired off a few emails and scrambled together maps and notebooks; hastily assembled a couple of tokens. I checked the forecast: heavy rain. This is how the best plans come together — an impulse, a necessity. I would leave early the following morning and celebrate Doris with a journey from her home and final resting place in Croydon to the edge of the cliff at Beachy Head.

The grey-block territories surrounding East Croydon

station must be the inspiration behind the quip that Croydon is 'like Manhattan built in Poland'. Boarding the 198 bus (final destination: SHRUBLANDS) I was struck by the anachronism of my efforts. So many of these buildings, these roads, the entire tram system that has become key to the place's pulse: neither my grandfather nor Doris nor my father, born here just before the war, would recognize any of it. I supposed they would be surprised by the people who joined me on the bus too — a couple of South American guys out for the day; an old Jamaican man and his 20-something English son; a Balkan woman in a headscarf. The bus handrails, the streetlights, bollards — most civic surfaces had been tagged with stickers by Crystal Palace Football Club supporters. I passed a squat utilitarian building, the Church of God Apostolic Mount Refuge Assembly.

The place through which the 198 bus cuts and dives is modern London. When Bob and Doris moved here in the late 1920s, it was neither. But there are still remnants of the Surrey suburb it once was. The stuccoed semis lining the widened streets, and the names of the spurs jutting off from the main drags: The Vale, The Glen.

I had determined that Doris left on the morning of

Friday 22nd July 1932 from her home in Kingscote Road. She would have walked or taken a bus from Addiscombe to East Croydon station, and there boarded a train bound for Eastbourne. At that end, I imagined her walking from the station to the top of Beachy Head. She arrived there in the late afternoon. I would do the same.

But before going to Kingscote Road I wanted to find her grave. I had exchanged emails with a man named Bernard, a volunteer at the church of St John the Evangelist in Shirley. I had found reference to Doris's interment at this church and noted a citation for the gravesite: H / 133 / 2nd. Bernard told me that, yes, I was right in thinking that St John's had a very large churchyard, and shouldn't expect to find a memorial just by wandering. But if this citation was correct, I could follow arcane instructions to find her: through the lychgate, left at the flagpole, six rows in and twelve paces and step back one, for Judas...

By the time the rain came barreling down, I was utterly lost. A clap of thunder accompanied the noon bell's ring, and a downpour. I huddled under a tree, beside Nora Mary Hersden 'Who fell asleep 2nd December 1950 — The Kindest Of All'. The graveyard was lined with avenues of trees and overseen by a huge building like a Suffolk wool church, its doors locked in a tip of the hat to the dangers of the modern world. I rearranged some outerwear and went back to counting rows and steps. Just as I was considering quitting to a dry café, the sun began to break through and I saw a stone that said 'Doris'.

It's a standard type of headstone — a book motif, open on its center spread:

> In cherished memory of DORIS dearly beloved wife of ROBERT HOPPER ... And of their son JOHN died 10th Feb. 1931, aged 2 years.

Speak their names

It was very calm, the rain still pattering. Swallows were banking above, and up on Shirley Church Road someone was sitting in their parked car playing a 'Sleng Teng' reggae track. I crouched before the names on the stones. 'Aged 2 years'. Less than a month beforehand, my son had turned the same age.

I had a photograph with me — a copy of a picture of Doris holding little John in the back garden of their home, the same garden in which she and Bob Hopper had been photographed. She is wearing a loose skirt-and-top combination, with slanted lines stitched across the top at a 45-degree angle. He has that determined overbite-smile of a two-year-old, pudgy and troublesome. I look at that photo cursed with the knowledge of what will come. He is so content, spilling out of his mother's arms, she joyful at containing him.

In my floundering, last-minute attempt to prepare for this journey, I had sent out an SOS to a set of friends asking for help — how to commemorate someone of whom I knew so little? I would go to Croydon and on to the Downs, to Beachy Head, but what could I do? The responses were many and varied: enjoy the food she would have eaten, the music she might have danced to.

I asked Adam the druid, hoping for a pagan ritual, but his advice was more simple: speak their names and they will never disappear. I placed the photograph in the wet grass before the gravestone and spoke their names aloud amidst the swallow-call: 'Dorothy Florence Stubbings, Dorothy Florence Greenin, Doris Greenin, Doris Hopper. John Hatton Hopper, Uncle John.'

Eastbourne has been engineered to funnel visitors down from the station through its streets, shops and cafes until they arrive at the seaside with its pier and promenade. But this particular summer Saturday had been interrupted by regular lashings of wind and rain. No one was around. I walked a mile and a half along the seafront, and encountered few more than a dozen people. The ice-cream stand grottos and seafront tourist vistas stood at the ready. Fresh flowers garnished the street-side planters, and the wide promenade was prepared for multitudes.

The night before my journey to Beachy Head, in sleepless online reading, I'd discovered a word, *kenopsia*: a term invented by The Dictionary of Obscure Sorrows for 'the eerie, forlorn atmosphere of a place that's usually bustling with people'. Halfway along the promenade was the Eastbourne Bandstand, a half-shell hovering above the shoreline. Its seating is part of the walk itself, the path scooting between rows of unfolded chairs set up for a concert that evening. By all appearances it was preparing for the gig — there was even music (Ed Sheeran) playing over the speakers. But there wasn't a soul to be seen: no one at the mixing desk, no one on or near the stage, no one behind it, every seat empty. Kenopsia: '…not just empty but hyper-empty, with a total population in the negative, who are so conspicuously absent they glow like neon signs.'

It isn't just the absent people but the absence of progress that glows brightly along Eastbourne's seafront. Everywhere signs are posted in denial of the new — posters for tribute bands and theatre revivals and salutes to bawdy seaside farce. One of the few people I did encounter was a man standing behind his 1930s-era convertible, dressed entirely in period garb, finishing a glass of wine before packing it back into a picnic set that was strapped to the car's rear. They flock to Eastbourne, the re-enactors — be they mods and rockers or Edwardian dandies.

Eastbourne halts suddenly where the Downs burst from the town. It feels incongruous against the tourist shops of the seafront that tame the island's edge with postcards, deckchairs and ice cream. The Downs rise from the end of a street as if untethering from the land.

I started walking the sharp incline up the side of the Head. Alongside the designated footpaths and photogenic heather are clumps of trees filled nightly with beer cans and campfires. Tracks veer off in every direction and, without warning, terminate above hundred-foot drops. Beachy Head is the kind of tourist spot that constantly denies its status. It is an unforgiving place, prone to weather dynamics and mood shifts unfelt just a few hundred meters to the east.

Doris climbed that route, I was sure of it; she walked past the same bursts of green and purple. Maybe she still did. It hardly seemed worth questioning the ghosts when the air was so thick with their hauntings. At Beachy Head, one cannot move for them; their wind-bursts, the taps at your shoulder on a deserted chalk path. Their clothes.

Hips against the cord People find them occasionally at the edge of the cliff at Beachy Head: the trig points of neatly folded clothes. A pair of trousers or a summery dress, perhaps a pair of socks; accoutrements such as a Bible or a bottle, a mobile phone. I've never seen them except in photographs — the Brighton artist Wendy Pye recreates them for a series of photographs called *Liminal*. The effect is purgatorial, raptured. The act of suicide at Beachy Head is terrible in part because it is so decisive. It involves travel, planning, careful consideration and ritual. I'd read about the clothes left at the cliff's edge, one of the strange traditions people seem to latch onto as their final moments near, shedding like a husk this last association with the land of the quick.

I saw Pye's photographs — a pair of tennis shoes inches from the edge — and I wondered about Doris's handbag.

The archive had continued to bear new fruits, and these reports from July 1932 read like tiny poems, each one consisting of only a few lines, yet densely packed with subtext.

'Holidaymakers at Beachy Head on Friday saw a young woman fall over the cliff edge to a ledge 400 feet below,' read the *Western Gazette*. She had no fractures, but severe head wounds. She was hauled up by the three coastguard men who descended from the cliff and lashed her to a stretcher, still conscious. 'In the woman's handbag was found the name and address: 'Doris Hopper, Addiscombe, Croydon."

Where was this handbag? Snagged on a tree root like a Warner Brothers cartoon? Fallen by her side, perfectly but precariously placed on the ledge? Did she clutch it while falling?

'Her husband arrived in Eastbourne last night.'

The shape of Doris's trip to the Downs came into view. She was alone — holidaymakers had seen her fall, but it was only through a note in her handbag that her identity came to light. Bob had come from Kingscote

Road later that night to be with her in care. She was injured, and badly. The papers played it down in the very short reports, saying that she suffered no broken bones and was expected to be fine, but the *Western Gazette* tells us that, 'the woman was suffering from severe head wounds.'

The cliffscape at Beachy Head is eroding rapidly, and always has been — this constant attrition is what keeps England's white cliffs white, fresh chalk constantly being revealed. As recently as 2000, massive landslides have radically altered the face of Beachy Head, that one destroying a landmark known for centuries as the Devil's Chimney. So there's no knowing the exact spot from which Doris fell or stepped. But if it still exists, it's likely to have been a point opposite the Beachy Head pub, where the sheerest drop is to be found.

There, her hips pressed against the cord warning people to go no further, was a woman with dyed-red hair and a pale face, her hands plunged into the pockets of her hoodie. At her feet was a bag — a handbag or very small pack, dropped on the grass near the edge. She stared out at the clouds, the sea, the horizon. I walked past her on my first circuit along the cliff's edge. I circled the promontory between the pub and the path to Belle Tout lighthouse and tried, in vain, to photograph the light. It was impossibly beautiful, butter-knife-spread light, shimmering off the sea and the sky and the chalk and the cow fields. When I walked past the woman again, she was still staring in the same spot, motionless. I was within six feet of her.

"Isn't this light amazing?" I said. No answer. "The light," I swept my hand like a preacher, "it's incredible tonight, isn't it?" She grunted in the affirmative, at least acknowledging that I'd spoken to her, and looked towards me briefly. My worries were not allayed. I kept half an eye in that direction while I moved ten meters along the shore to a series of wooden crosses, each about a foot tall and wide. I put my bag down, dropped it on the grass near the edge, and took out another photograph: Doris and Bob in the garden, happy. Hunting around, I found two lumps of chalk, big ones protruding from the ground. I reached over and placed the photograph near the crosses, weighed it down at opposite corners and repeated Doris's names, trying to imagine her in that light, summery, art deco outfit, holding her hat, walking this same perimeter.

Closing up my bag, a short, balding man with a pair of binoculars around his neck approached me and smiled.

"What do you think, is that a ship out that way, or can we see Europe?" He had the hint of a German accent. He held out the binoculars with a pursed smile and winking eye. It was a massive ship, a ship one might mistake for a continent, but that wasn't the point. I hadn't realized how obvious these probing questions were, these verbal sonar pings sent out to determine another's intentions. I also hadn't realized how many behaviors seem suspicious on Beachy Head.

When I walked past the red-haired woman again, her friends were walking up towards her at their appointed meeting spot. She was waving and smiling. Nothing she'd done would have raised suspicion in a professional. Nothing I did, either. But I'm glad people are looking out for one another, even if we usually get it wrong.

Stories can change A few years ago, I met a man named Ross Hardy who had a vision. In July 2003, Hardy was pastoring at a small, non-denominational, 'free' church in Wannock, at the northern suburban end of Eastbourne, near Jevington, an area small enough to not register on many maps. It was a Sunday, and he was looking for a message — something to speak about at his Church of the Way that morning —

and he slipped into a state of altered consciousness.

"I believe God gave me a vision. It was like a daydream; it lasted about half an hour — the vision of two people patrolling Beachy Head, reaching out to those who were depressed and suicidal. It was a vision that really burned in my heart, and from that point onwards, I worked to get this team into place."

Hardy couldn't shake the vision, and for more than a year dedicated his life, his work, his reserves of energy and cash into making it a reality.

"I couldn't get rid of it, and believe me, I tried. I don't like heights, I'm a terrible organizer, and I'm not too good at talking to people one-to-one. All of the things I needed for this job were … not my thing."

A year and a week after Hardy's vision, Beachy Head Chaplaincy took its first patrol of the cliff top. They arrived a little bit before 7pm — and by 7.30pm, they had encountered their first jumper. It's not that there's *always* someone out there, prowling the edge, but it probably feels that way to the men and women who patrol: the despondent, the missing, the angry who have stormed out muttering threats about Beachy Head. When a man in Eastbourne or a woman in Croydon goes missing, sometimes having mentioned the cliff in the past, the Chaplaincy gets a call and adds a search to their regular patrols. They walk the Downs, scan the pubs, drive the byways of Sussex looking for signs.

During its 12 years on the edge, the Chaplaincy has conducted an average of two searches per day. They have engaged a potential jumper two out of three days, negotiating the majority of them into living. (It's mostly talking, being there, but not always: the Chaplaincy reserves the right to physically stop someone from jumping, if circumstances demand it.) But it doesn't work every time.

"I've been involved in hundreds of interventions in some capacity," Hardy told me. "I've seen people end their life. It has an impact. As a Christian team, we rely on the Grace of God to carry us. But sometimes it's really tough. You can get very angry at someone for making that choice — and for not accepting your help. It's heartbreaking when you meet families, see families torn apart. Often, the people ending their lives think they're doing their family a favor. Yet you see these families suffering afterwards. They'd do anything they could to have their loved one back.

"The danger is that, over time, your heart can harden, and we need to have our hearts open — that's how the negotiation process works. We *do* care for them. We want to help them. It's not just a job."

Beachy Head is the event horizon of the English mind — neither land, nor sea, just the edge of being and beyond it, nothingness — it has nearly a thousand years behind it. It is engrained, but that doesn't mean that a new story cannot be told; cannot evolve. The chalk erodes day by day, year by year, always leaving a new white sheen.

I'd made the journey to Beachy Head out of a sense of duty to Doris's story. I wanted to remember her, wanted to bring her back from disappearance. But I had failed to recognize the flaw in my strategy: I was trying to *know* her. I was guessing at her path and her reasoning, groping for answers and a resolution. An ending, if not necessarily a happy one. But the act of remembering — the dignity I sought to give her — came through something harder to resolve. It was the act of being there, of recognizing the traces she has left. It was the act of speaking a name.

I hope that the evening she went over the edge was like the evening on which I visited. The wash of light, the

vagaries of the sounds — people, birds, dogs — all set to
an ocean hum one might play to a child to lull her into
sleep. The lowering sun backlit the Downs, and it seemed
I could see them in their entirety. The chalk breathed with
visions; a castle of light and cloud in the distance might
have been Winchester, beyond kingdoms of cows and
lines and circles. It was there, at the end of an Old Road
followed from memory to memory across a strange land.

Like a
restora-
tion
That night I slept in my own bed, alone in my home, a
19th-century farm-worker's cottage a hundred miles from
Beachy Head. It rattled in the East Anglian wind. I slept
deeply with no child to listen out for, but I dreamt, not of
Doris and not of John, but of my own son, Thomas. And
of his own map of this old, weird Albion.

When he and I walk, he recognizes each corner of
a field, each subtle shift in the landscape — through a
kissing gate, over a stile, into the field of beans or of cows
or of wheat — by a story. He speaks these aloud, stories
about who has passed by there before: "Mummy, Daddy,
Thomas … Grannie, Thomas … Ma, Pa, Daddy, Thomas."

It will stop soon — his grammar has already
outgrown it. But for now it feels like a restoration. It's so

natural to understand the world by these narratives; to annotate our landscapes with shared memories, be that through song or story, a mark scrawled in the chalk or the wheat or on the map, a home that carries with it the ghosts of those who have slept there before. This visible world isn't even the half of it. There is something older, something weirder. It lingers.

ACKNOWLEDGEMENTS

I am, first and foremost, grateful to all the individuals who are named in this book as my guides on the Downs, each of whom offered wisdom and wit along our travels. A number of others have acted as guides in their own ways, including CL Brown, Louis Buckley, Nathan Burr, Shirley Collins, John Copper, Valmai Goodyear, Jim Jupp, Sharron Kraus, Frances Lord, Nick Medford, Robert O'Mahoney, Mark Pilkington and Strange Attractor Press, Wendy Pye, Adam Ranger, and Chris Tod and Steyning Museum. I am thankful for their inspiration, assistance and insight. My relatives were generous with their stories and memories, for which I am indebted. Writers whose work has proved invaluable include Peter Brandon, Janet Pennington, Diana Souhami and Joseph Pearce. Greil Marcus is a lasting influence and inspired this book's title. The concept for this project owes a great deal to Rachel Lichtenstein, Sukhdev Sandhu and our colleagues from the Arvon Foundation and Totleigh Barton.

I am grateful for the work of Leah Fusco and Mairead Dunne, whose images accompany this project.

Tom Chivers of Penned in the Margins has believed in and supported me throughout the process of creating this book. I am thankful to both Tom and his colleague James Trevelyan for helping to bring *The Old Weird Albion* into the world.

Paul and Helen Hopper gave me the gift of their own fascination with the world; I thank them for their lifelong support and encouragement. I am grateful to Thomas for his immense love and patience. Finally, this work could never have happened without the love, support, enthusiasm and hard work of Lucy Greeves. 'There is a garden where our hearts converse...'

— JH